BRIDAL COUTURE

BRIDAL COUTURE

Fine Sewing Techniques for Wedding Gowns and Evening Wear

SUSAN KHALJE

Published by

 **krause
publications**

700 E. State Street • Iola, WI 54990-0001
Telephone: 715/445-2214

Please call or write for our free catalog of publications.
Our toll-free number to place an order or obtain a free catalog is 800-258-0929 or please use our
regular business telephone 715-445-2214 for editorial comment and further information.

Designed by Tony Jacobson
Color photographs by June Chaplin, Baltimore
Color photographs styled by Michael Ruddie
Black-and-white photographs by Michael DeFilippi
Illustrations by Mary Ellen Szper

Manufactured in the United States of America
Library of Congress Cataloging-in-Publication Data
Khalje, Susan
    Bridal couture : fine sewing techniques for wedding gowns and
evening wear / Susan Khalje.
      p.   cm.
    Includes index.
    ISBN 0-8019-8757-1 (pbk.)
    1. Dressmaking.   2. Wedding costume.   I. Title.
TT560.K49   1997
646.4'7—dc21   97-325
                                                                CIP

1 2 3 4 5 6 7 8 9 0   6 5 4 3 2 1 0 9 8 7

Acknowledgments

Grateful thanks are given to the following for their generous assistance:

David Aitken
Amy Anderson
The Baltimore Museum of Art
Jane Brochin
Jeff Conti
Cylburn Arboretum
Janet David
Evergreen House
Rula Ghani
Isaac Jones
Doris Katz
Khalje Oriental Rug Gallery
La Terra
New Systems Bakery
Pearl Gallery
Suzanne Rafferty and Mark Fabian
Linda Rhinehart and Gemme
Arlynne Stark
Lucia Stefanescu
Sarah Veblen
The Walters Art Gallery

Thanks to the following clients who were kind enough to lend me their gowns:

Amy Chapman
Amy Crichton
Holly Hannon
Barbara Hart
Beth Kiesel
Kathleen Krach
Stacy Peddy
Shelly Pinkner
Kerri Pursley
Susan Rizzi
Jackie Sawiris
Sarah Schweizer
Sara Slater
Janet Ward

Enormous gratitude is due the following:

My editors at Chilton: Robbie Fanning, for giving life to the project, and Susan Keller, for her thoughtful counsel, patience, and good humor. An author couldn't ask for a better editor

And my team:
Michael DeFilippi, photographer, for his skill and his calm and professional approach
Mary Ellen Szper, illustrator, for her careful work and attention to detail
Michael Ruddie, photo stylist, for his endless creativity and talent in all manners artistic
June Chaplin, photographer, for sharing her artistry, her ideas, and her sense of humor; I could not have contemplated, let alone completed, this project without her valued input and support

I am most of all grateful to my family:

to my parents, for their lifelong support and encouragement
to my mother, for all the hours spent proofreading
to my father, for his masterful assistance with the computer
to my twin sister Karen, for her unfailing belief in this project
to my children, Soraya and Sharif, and most especially to my husband Qadir—for their enthusiasm and patience

Special thanks to my sewing friends:

Kathleen Spike, who insisted upon the need for this book
Sandra Betzina, who enthusiastically embraced the idea
Anna McNaught, a kindred spirit in sewing and so much else
Delores Rhody, for her longtime support
Mirjana Freilich, for encouraging my teaching efforts
Catherine Stephenson, who shares my passion for the couture
Roberta Carr, whose efforts and enthusiasm have introduced countless sewers to the world of couture
Claire Shaeffer, whose quality of work and scope of knowledge is truly inspirational

I must also thank my colleagues in the Professional Association of Custom Clothiers; it is through the efforts of PACC that our profession is alive and well and has a future.

This book is dedicated to three women:

To Hilda Bennett, my late grandmother, to whom sewing was a natural and beloved part of life. I thank her for setting that example.

To Marian Anderson, my aunt, for showing me the joy of incorporating creativity into one's life. I thank her for all her encouragement.

And to Olga Holzmuller, the Bez of Chez Cez et Bez, the most skilled dressmaker I've ever known. I thank her for the generosity with which she shared her knowledge.

CONTENTS

OREWORD

A wedding is one of the most significant events in a woman's life. A celebration filled with time-honored traditions, splendor, and solemnity, it celebrates a rite of passage and marks the beginning of a new life. Equally important for the older woman attended by her children and grandchildren as for the young woman marrying for the first time, it is a time of shared joy, a symbol of faith and hope for future generations.

The wedding is the fantasy made real. It is a magical, fairytale occasion that begins in the dreams of little girls. The principal roles are played by the bride and her prince charming. In reality, it is the bride's day; and it is she who will steal the show with her radiance and magnificent costume.

The wedding dress is unlike any other element of fashion. A magical symbol of love and romance, fantasy and splendor, sentiment and tradition, it represents the expectations of future happiness and eternal bliss. For hundreds of years and in every society, brides have worn elaborate ceremonial robes that ranged from richly colored and brightly embroidered native costumes to royal robes woven with threads of gold and silver and embellished with precious metals and jewels.

Many of today's most popular wedding customs began during the reign of Queen Victoria. For her marriage to Prince Albert of Saxe-Coburg in 1840, the young monarch chose a simple white dress. Fabricated from heavy silk satin woven in Spitalfields, England, and trimmed with handmade Honitan lace, it was austere when compared to the elaborate, ostentatious gowns of silver tissue worn by her predecessors.

Designed to promote the well-established English textile industries, the Queen's choice was an enormous success. Stylish and elegant, the dress created a demand, which continues even today, for beautiful white wedding gowns with an abundance of lace trims.

The invention of the sewing machine in 1846 had a profound effect on dressmaking: Instead of making dressmaking faster and simpler, it encouraged the use of more elaborate trims. By the end of the century when the passion for decoration reached its peak, wedding gowns were elaborately trimmed with a variety of ornate embellishments, including fringe, braid, pleating, shirring, and laces.

One of the most popular wedding traditions—the rhyme "something old, something new, something borrowed, something blue, a sixpence (penny) in your shoe" is, by many accounts, another Victorian invention. Based on a variety of religious and pagan sources, each line is significant.

"Something old" represents the past and is usually a family heirloom—a Bible, a piece of jewelry, or a bit of antique lace sewn into the bridal gown. "Something new" represents the future and is generally the wedding gown itself. Based on the superstition that happiness rubs off, "something borrowed" is frequently a handkerchief or veil borrowed from a happily married relative or friend. "Something blue" represents purity, love, and fidelity, and dates back to the time of the ancient Israelites. Generally worn as a ribbon or on a garter, many believe blue brings good luck. "A sixpence in your shoe" is a wish for a life of good fortune and prosperity.

Designed to wish the bride good luck, there are many additional superstitions employed in haute couture workrooms. One of the most popular is to sew a strand of hair from a happily married needleworker into the gown's hem. Others include sewing a small horseshoe into the hem or on the waist stay. The horseshoe, which is silver or simply cardboard covered with blue satin ribbon, is supposed to ward off evil spirits and bring good luck.

One of the joys of sewing is that you can establish your own traditions and interpret your own fantasies. Bridal Couture includes everything you need to know to create a wedding gown that is both timely and timeless. It is filled with numerous photographs that convey the beauty, luxurious fabrication, and fine construction of Susan Khalje's designs. And, with Susan's expert guidance, you can translate your dream gown into a reality.

Best wishes for a beautiful wedding and a long and happy marriage.

Claire B. Shaeffer

$\mathscr{P}$REFACE

I remember walking in downtown Baltimore one day with my mother when I was a little girl. We turned a corner, and I looked up to see a wedding party coming out of a church. I begged my mother if we could wait to see the bride. We did, of course, and when she appeared, I was speechless— she was wearing the most beautiful dress I'd ever seen. I always drew my own outfits for my paper dolls, and when we got home, I tried to design a wedding gown as beautiful as the one I'd seen for my favorite paper doll. Wedding gowns seemed magical to me from that day on.

The wedding itself, and the wedding gown, are part of a fairy tale, but fairy tales need to be grounded in reality if they are to come true, and this book— a wish book—will inspire the bride and the dressmaker alike. It will acquaint you thoroughly with the process of sewing a wedding gown, presenting techniques that can be applied to all fine sewing projects. Couture techniques lend themselves perfectly to projects of this scope: important dresses, worn at important moments, deserving of the finest of fabrics used in the finest of ways. Anyone with a solid base of sewing and fitting skills will be able to take their sewing to a new level.

Included are:

- a portfolio of gowns I've made over the years; their range of styles and fabrication will inspire you
- a look at common, and not-so-common, choices for fabrication: fabrics and laces in all their wonderful variety, how and why to choose them, and how to use them
- the equipment and supplies you need to have on hand

- a detailed look at the concept of the muslin: a mock-up of the gown in inexpensive fabric, and an essential part of the couture process, in which design, proportion and fit are perfected; it will allow you to proceed, confidently, to create the gown in the fashion fabric
- a thorough explanation of all the inner support a gown needs, from underlining to boning to stays, from the obvious to the subtle
- a comprehensive look at the construction process, in which the components of the gown are first created, then joined together
- a close look at the construction, step by step, of four gowns, from start to finish; among them, they present a broad range of styles, fabrication and techniques
- and, finally, a glossary of sewing techniques, a select number of valuable and hard-to-find resources, a list of books to further inspire you, and even a pronunciation guide to the wonderful and exotically named fabrics and terms which are central to these gowns

All the big questions are answered: fabrication, engineering, inner support and construction, as well as the little ones: the finishing details and the final touches, to make a special gown even more special.

What led me to write this book was my own search for information, for techniques, for encouragement. I wanted to know what I was doing right, and what I could do better. I've studied new gowns, vintage gowns, mothers' gowns, grandmothers' gowns, ball gowns,

haute couture gowns, gowns from discount houses, gowns in private collections, gowns in books, gowns in museums. I've learned from all of them. I've seen what works and, often, what doesn't work. In my own sewing, I've learned while creating gowns, from the simple to the elaborate, from commercial patterns and from my own designs, from the straightforward to the challenging. I've learned what to do and what not to do. I've gone from being terrified to buy expensive lace (let alone cut into it and do anything with it) to feeling confident in my choices and in working with them. I've gone from making gowns with hardly any inner support at all, praying that they'd stay up long enough for the ceremony to take place, to constructing gowns that are well-engineered, comfortable, and secure to wear. I've gone from hoping that something might work to knowing what will work. My mistakes—and I've made and learned from them all—were valuable, and my experimentation has led to successful solutions. This is the information I'd like to share with you.

Your entire way of sewing may be transformed, or you may choose simply to incorporate a new technique or two into your sewing repertoire; either way, you'll become a participant in the art of fine sewing. The spirit of couture, with its rich background and strong sense of tradition, will guide you, inspire you, and delight you.

So, whether you're sewing a wedding gown that will be the centerpiece of a celebration for hundreds of people, or simply creating something wonderful for your own pleasure, this is the perfect opportunity to make it special. And maybe there will be a little girl watching, enchanted, dreaming her own dreams…

INTRODUCTION

"When it is done properly, haute couture is at once a state of mind, an intellectual and artistic choice, a social and political expression, an aesthetic attitude, a commitment to effort and progress, a struggle against the banal, the mundane, a tool of communication; a means, if you will, of provoking thought, emotion, and desire."

—*Christian Lacroix*[*]

Haute couture—the very words transport us into the atmosphere of luxury and elegance of the world's premiere fashion salons. The creations, the fantasies, the otherworldly confections uphold the standards of design and workmanship to which the rest of us aspire. Haute couture translates, literally, as "high sewing," or sewing on the highest level, and it is nothing less than that. Decades of devotion to craft, of uncompromising standards in fabrication, design, fit, and technique have brought the couture to where it is today: the highest expression of the dressmaker's art.

The hours involved in the creation of an haute couture garment are impressive, a testimony to the level of quality expected and demanded. Wearing an haute couture garment is, of course, a luxury, but creating one is a luxury as well, in terms of design, scope, proportions, material, and the time spent in its creation. An haute couture day dress typically takes one hundred hours to create, and gowns can take many times that.

Haute couture specifically refers to the work produced in the ateliers (workrooms) of certain designers in Paris (who subscribe to very stringent guidelines in order to be so named) and

Rome. Couture, which is simply the French word for sewing, refers to garments constructed, with the finest of sewing techniques, in anyone's atelier. The standards are much the same: a devotion to creativity, the use of the finest of fabrics, flawless fit, sound engineering, and technical perfection.

Although the goals of the haute couture are lofty, they are rooted in down-to-earth sewing techniques. It is earthly ingredients which produce such heavenly results. And what the haute couture designer and the dressmaker have in common is a love of the process, from the initial design to the final stitch.

Couture, beyond the rarefied image of the word itself, is, as much as anything, a decision-making process. The dressmaker is constantly thinking, weighing possibilities, and problem solving, knowing that there are multiple workable solutions to any dressmaking challenge and that inherent in the art is the process of trial and error and the knowledge that something less than perfect can be redone.

In practical terms, couture translates into careful, logical, well-thought-out applications of solid technique. Whether in the House of Chanel or in one's own workroom, the components are the same:

- fabrication: the finest of luxury fabrics, used alone or in unexpected and striking combinations
- design: what does the gown say as it communicates through fabric, color, proportion, balance, innovation, creativity, and sometimes even whimsy
- fit and proportion: multiple fittings in muslin and adjustments to design and proportion which are both subtle and marked
- engineering and inner structure: coming to very practical terms with the "architecture of movement," as Balmain called it
- workmanship: impeccable craftsmanship of the highest level and painstaking attention to detail, with much of the sewing done by hand

These ingredients must all be present for the gown to become, as Christian Lacroix says, "a means of provoking thought, emotion, and desire."

It is the dressmaker's challenge to weave the elements together, to base fantasy in reality, to create an otherworldly garment with solid technical skills. In so doing, one develops an appreciation of the art, a devotion to the process, and a love of the craft.

---

[*] *"Quand elle est faite comme il se doit, la haute couture est à la fois un état d'esprit, un choix intellectuel et artistique, une expression sociale et politique, une allure esthétique, une volonté d'effort et de progrès, un combat contre le banal, le quotidien, un outil de communication, une machine enfin à provoquer la réflexion, l'émotion, le désir."*
— Christian Lacroix, in *Paris Match*, February 1996

INSPIRATION

A Portfolio of Gowns by Susan Khalje

"*I want to give an image of dreams...It's a designer's role to make people dream. The message is very, very clear: beauty.*"

—Gianni Versace

The bodice of this gown is covered with daisy-patterned Austrian cotton guipure lace; its flowered border is placed so that it appears to continue around the top of the bodice and the top of the sleeves. The multilayered tulle skirt is cut so that there is no fullness at the waist.

This romantic pink satin ball gown has a long, flower-trimmed detachable train which hooks under a built-in bustle. Flowers appear everywhere in this gown: subtly, in the patterns of the antique lace on the bodice and lower sleeves; more dramatically at the base of the upper part of the sleeves, at the sides of the skirt, and on the train.

4

The highly textured silk douppioni is matched with metallic trim, both new and antique. The metal sequins, which are held in place with tiny silver beads, give the appearance of having been scattered over the gown.

This is a gown for dramatic entrances, its long silhouette contrasting with the full, sparkly, flower-trimmed detachable train. The train has a built-in bustle, and its layers of tulle are generously sprinkled with sequins.

Simplicity is the hallmark of this beautiful gown with its Alençon lace–covered bodice and sleeves and its tulle skirt. More complicated is the inner structure: Generous amounts of boning create a flattering silhouette and shape the basque waist, while eight layers of tulle cover a taffeta underskirt.

Silk shantung forms a lustrous background for the heavily pearled Alençon lace in this traditional gown. The patterns of the lace are carefully matched on the bodice and sleeves, and the waistline falls toward the back of the skirt, its sloping line accented by a heavily pearled trim.

A number of independent elements come together to create this gracious gown: the luscious, puffy sleves; the tightly fitted, low-cut bodice with its shirring and row of pearl buttons down the back; and the full silk shantung skirt trimmed with three rows of bias-cut silk douppioni.

This soft and pretty gown has whispers of color: The bodice underlining, the sleeve lining, the tinted Alençon trim at the bottom of the skirt, and the silk roses at the shoulders are all the softest shade of pink.

The theme here is the color peach—it is echoed in the iridescent sequins that are heavily applied to the ecru lace, in the peach shantung of the gown, and in the peach tulle overskirts. The inner layer of tulle is scattered with sequins, creating a more subtle effect than placing them on the top layer of tulle. The ruffle at the neckline (called a crumb-catcher) is cut on the bias and underlined with net.

A simple and sophisticated linen dress that echoes the style of Audrey Hepburn, this gown uses Swiss linen in two forms. The bodice, which dips to a deep V in the back, is made from allover cutwork linen, and the skirt is gathered from a single length of the matching cut-work-bordered linen.

Here cotton lace, which almost appears to be hand-crocheted, combines with douppioni; the scallops on the border of the lace complement the scallops on the double-layered skirt. The color of the bow is a surprise, and the bright buttons emphasize this burst of color.

This sophisticated top is made from heavily beaded, very firm Alençon lace, which is sturdy enough to function on its own without an underlining. The sleeves are bell-shaped, and the bodice, which cuts lower in the back than in the front, flares away from the body.

This dress is very linear, in both fabrication and style. Everything in it echoes strong lines—from the cotton faille with its prominent horizontal texture, used in the body of the gown, to the striped silk organza of the band collar (cut on the bias), to the clean, elegant, spare silhouette itself.

The skirt of this gentle guipure lace and silk shantung gown softly sweeps the floor. The fullness and shape of the sleeves, the scoop of the neckline, the circumference and length of the skirt, and the position of the dropped waist all blend to create a well-balanced gown.

This is a well-pro-
portioned, gentle
gown with neck
and wrist ruffles
and seven gradu-
ated tiers of soft
chiffon. A length
of mauve antique
velvet ribbon
forms a soft bow
at the waist,
adding a subtle
note of color.

Glass beads cover the lace on the heavily-boned bustier of this ensemble. The separate silk shantung skirt is underlined with silk organza, and silk flowers accentuate the gathers that appear intermittently on the lower tier of the skirt.

FABRICATION

"I come in. I'm going to sketch, I'm going to drape, I don't know what I'm going to do. Design is an unknown. From fabric that is very flat, it just suddenly takes form and shape and meaning. When I don't have any idea, I pick up fabric and then I start working with it and something happens. Design is a revelation to me. It's like taking something that is not alive and giving it form, shape, substance, and life."

—Geoffrey Beene

Fabrics

As any designer will tell you, it is often the fabric which sparks the initial inspiration and provides the creative impetus for an entire project. Dressmakers, too, are blessed with a special talent for seeing the possibilities within a piece of fabric. The dressmaker's vision, combined with solid technical knowledge of the fabric's personality and idiosyncrasies, is an essential component of any successful gown.

ASPECTS OF FABRICATION

Fabrication—that is, all of the fabric elements used in a garment—contributes to the overall effect of the gown and, at the same time, underpins it in practical, structural ways. Fashion fabric and lace create the texture, sweep, and feel of a gown. When more than one fabric is used, the interplay of complementary or contrasting fabrics becomes part of the design. Also, there can be a great deal of fabric—yards and yards—and the sheer amount of it makes a statement. Underlinings and linings add support and weight, playing a necessary part in the visual impact of the gown.

Fashion Fabric

Design and fabric go hand in hand. Each component of the gown has different design requirements and thus different fabric requirements. The skirt, for example, is often where the fabric has the greatest impact—partly because of the amount of fabric used there, partly because of the motion of the skirt. A skirt must flow, cling, float, rustle, sweep, or envelop. None of this can occur without the proper fabric. The bodice and the sleeves, on the other hand, are relatively static. It is usually form, not motion, that is essential to their design needs.

The fashion fabrics of the gown will, if well chosen, chart the course for success in form, function, and movement—that essential equation of a well-designed gown. Choosing the right fabric not only serves the designer's needs, it also encourages the wearer to understand and feel the designer's vision. When the wearer of the gown is enfolded in yards of richly lustrous satin, she starts to feel practically regal. Waves of gossamer silk chiffon help conjure a floating, fairy-like feeling. It's a magical combination: The designer chooses the right fabric and uses it well, and the wearer benefits from the successful melding of design and fabrication.

Fabrics: **top row:** *pale yellow polyester organza, peach moiré;* **middle row:** *embroidered linen, embellished silk taffeta, metallic organza (skirt) with silk ribbon chiffon (shawl), ribbon-trimmed tulle;* **bottom row:** *lace-trimmed silk shantung, pink and gold silk taffeta, ecru silk damask, blue polyester satin, grape silk douppioni. (See larger photo on pages 22 and 23.)*

Underlining

Although never seen on the finished garment, the underlining (sometimes referred to as the backing) plays a critical role in a gown's success. The underlining is hand-basted to the fashion fabric and the two are treated thereafter as one. By adding strength to the fashion fabric, the underlining adds shape to the garment. The fabric is still the fabric, but more so, thanks to the underlining.

Underlining can fill out pleats and gathers, pad seams, and help strengthen the base on which lace and other embellishments will be applied. It allows the garment to be hemmed invisibly, lessens wrinkling, prevents stretching and bagging, and can be used to whiten a white, intensify a pastel, or make a transparent fabric opaque. Its roles are endless.

Underlining must be chosen with care, and often different underlinings are used in different parts of the garment. The bodice, for example, might need a firm layer, or several layers, of underlining to help it support a heavy skirt and sleeves, as well as camouflage boning; the same gown's lightweight taffeta skirt would be perfectly complemented by a silk organza underlining. Experimentation, careful observation, trial and error and remembering what's worked in the past are the keys to choosing the right underlinings. Silk organza will add crisp, lightweight support, cotton batiste will add soft support, poly-cotton batiste will be too thick and heavy for most skirts but will help firm up a bodice, as will muslin, crinoline, and even flannel.

Don't underestimate the role of the underlining and the help that it can give; along with beautiful design and quality fashion fabric, it is one of your biggest allies in the process of creating the perfect gown.

Fabric Weave and Fiber

Knowing how a fabric is woven will help you assess a fabric's characteristics and behavior (discussed in more detail later in this section). All fabrics are woven with two sets of yarns: the warp yarns (which run vertically on the loom), and the weft, or filling, yarns (which run horizontally on the loom). These two sets of yarns can be exactly the same (in fiber content, thickness of yarn and amount of twist), or they can be quite different.

The fiber content of the yarns used (natural, synthetic, or a combination) also plays a critical role in the fabric's behavior. Satin, taffeta, moiré, shantung, crepe, organza—these names all refer to the type of weave, not the fiber content. Silk organza behaves differently from polyester organza, silk shantung behaves differently from polyester shantung, and silk satin couldn't be more different from acetate satin.

While cost is usually the first indicator of quality fabric, many synthetics may be substituted for their costlier counterparts. If you are operating under budget constraints, consider what you will gain and lose by choosing a synthetic version of your preferred fabric. Silks breathe, cooperate, and dye beautifully. They are predictable, but at the same time flexible. Synthetic versions may prove disappointing. On the other hand, if you need a particular weight, color, texture, or opacity in a fabric, be sure to consider all combinations of fibers and weave. In the Glamorous Blue Gown in Part IV (see page 127), I was able to match a given color only by using a number of synthetics together.

ASSESSING FASHION FABRICS

A number of fabrics will be forever and always associated with wedding gowns and evening wear, and rightly so. The best of them are wonderful to look at, wonderful to work with, and wonderful to wear. However, for all their otherworldly charm and heavenly appeal, these fabrics must be used in skillful and logical ways to achieve the desired effects. A clear understanding of their strengths and weaknesses—as well as of their content and makeup—is the first step in creating a magical end result.

In this section, I offer my observations about the most commonly used

General Guidelines for Evaluating Fabric

Your fabric can be your best ally and a delight to work with or your worst enemy—a foe you must battle at every step of the project. Fortunately, you can tame difficult fabrics and make tricky fabrics more cooperative if you know what to expect from them. As you learn the specific qualities of luxury fabrics, ask yourself these general questions to help you make informed decisions.

Imperfections. Are there any imperfections that you'll need to work around? Slubs and stripes are a natural feature of many textured silks, but a prominent stripe in a conspicuous place, such as the bustline or skirt center, can be distracting.

Grain. Is the grain straight? Can it be straightened?

Quantity. Is there enough fabric on the bolt to cut out the entire gown (plus a little extra fabric for good measure)? Fabric on another bolt may not come from the same dye lot and thus the color may be ever-so-slightly different.

Direction. Does the fabric have a right and wrong side? Is there a directional (that is, up and down) pattern? Remember directional patterns can be obvious or very subtle.

Motif. If there are prominent motifs, as in a damask, how are they placed? What size are they? How will they be arranged on the bodice, skirt, sleeves, or hem?

Sewing and Pressing. Which thread type and size is appropriate for the fabric? Which needle size and presser foot should be used? Does the fabric press easily or with effort? What is the ideal temperature for pressing? Can the fabric take steam or moisture? Will the fabric shrink? Is there a noticeable crease from having been folded on the bolt? Will the crease press out?

special-occasion fabrics. Experiment with these fabrics. As you become familiar with them, you will begin to envision how they will best serve your design. You'll also want to keep in mind several practical considerations. How will each fabric be underlined, seamed, finished, lined, hemmed, fastened? Can ornamentation be applied to the fabric? Do the fabric choices fit into your budget? Would a smaller amount of a superior fabric be better than a larger amount of an inferior fabric? With time, patience, care, technique, skill, experimentation, and experience, you will find the perfect fabrics and use them in wonderful ways.

Satin

Satin is the most stately fabric of all—with its pearl-like luster, its soft strength, and its ability to convey magnificence by its very presence. Although gorgeous when used alongside other fabrics, satin is glorious by itself—soft as a kitten yet full of oomph. It is the perfect combination of boundless surface appeal and quiet power. It is the diva of gown fabrics.

Although satins vary widely in weight, luster, and fiber content, they are all woven the same way. Most of the filling yarns, which are barely twisted, are carried on the surface of the fabric; these are the "floats," so often referred to when speaking of satin. These low-twist yarns give satin its luster and softness, but they also make its surface delicate and prone to snagging. Since most of the yarn "floats" on the surface and little of it interlocks with the base, or warp, satin ravels easily. If you prefer less luster, consider peau de soie, a medium-weight, matte-finish satin weave fabric, which behaves much like the more lustrous satins.

Fiber content of satin varies widely, and combinations of fibers are common. Silk-faced satin, for example, in which silk fibers are woven on a polyester base, is a wonderful alternative to pure silk satins. Pure polyester satins are also workable choices, mimicking many of the qualities of the silks.

Satin…combines beautifully with lace; —works well with a silk organza underlining; organza's stiffness fills out folds and pleats without weighing down satin; —looks beautiful when softly folded; —has substantial fullness that is well controlled by knife pleats, box pleats, and inverted box pleats; —can be unwieldy when gathered; —water spots, especially if a pure silk or silk-blend; —snags, soils, puckers, and ravels easily (see handling tips in "Special Care for Satin"); — is slippery to work with and sew; —glazes when pressed without a pressing cloth.

Special Treatment for Satin

Although gorgeous to look at and hold, satin is very fussy and finicky to work with, demanding special attention to such details as pin placement, seam finishes, and even storage. The exquisite results that are possible make every bit of extra effort more than worthwhile. The following are some helpful hints for handling this fabric.

Handling. It doesn't take much to snag satin's smooth surface, so be sure needles, pins, shears, and even your hands are perfectly smooth before they touch it. (Here's an old-fashioned trick to help smooth rough hands: Mix a teaspoon of sugar with a teaspoon of oil, rub the mixture briskly over your hands for a minute or two, and then rinse your hands with soap and water.) Carefully place rough trims and buttons. A jeweled button, for example, will roughen a satin-bound buttonhole. Instead, position a nonfunctioning bound buttonhole and decorative button over a covered snap.

Storing. Keep uncut fabric on a cardboard tube; folds are difficult to remove, and satin's soft fibers attract dirt along fold lines. Store a partially constructed gown inside out on a clip-style hanger (attach by a skirt's seam allowance, for example) to prevent abrasion, soiling, and wrinkling.

Pinning. Place pins in seam allowances; marks may be left when pins are removed.

Cutting and Marking. Use a nap, or directional, layout for cutting out garment pieces; satin has a very subtle nap. And cut long, vertical seams very slightly off grain to reduce puckering when the garment is stitched. Always mark the underlining, not the satin itself; a tracing wheel will cut satin's delicate fibers.

Stitching. Hand baste with silk thread for fittings; ripped-out machine stitches will show. Baste carefully and closely; satin tends to slip when being stitched. When stitching seams, hold satin taut to minimize puckering, and zigzag seam allowances to help control raveling, especially along horizontal edges. If you're using a zipper closing, hand pick the zipper or insert an invisible one.

Finishing Seams. Hand overcast long seam allowances or bind them with a Hong Kong finish; if using a lining, simply trim seam allowances carefully.

Hemming. Hem to the underlining only; it is impossible to hide stitches in satin. Alternatively, bind the bottom edge with narrow satin bias strips or matching (and lighter-weight) crepe de chine or charmeuse.

Pressing. To avoid glazing, always use a pressing cloth when pressing satin. Use strips of brown paper under the seam allowances to guard against seam allowance show-through.

Shantung

Lovely on its own and a perfect partner for lace, design details, and ornamentation, shantung is perhaps the most versatile and widely used of the traditional gown fabrics. Although soft and lightweight, it is easily strengthened with underlining. It gathers beautifully, it wrinkles little, and there's nothing temperamental about working with it or wearing it. It is available in silk and polyester. Silk shantung's texture comes from slubbed filling yarns, and occasionally, a bit of cocoon (which can be avoided during layout or picked out with a needle or pin).

Shantung…has a moderate sheen that is complemented by its texture; —is available in different weights (your choice of weight will affect your choice of underlining); —has prominent horizontal lines that are obvious if the garment isn't perfectly placed on the grain; —works well with organza and lightweight batiste underlinings; —looks beautiful with lace along the hem; —doesn't slip during layout and cutting; —is easy to press (synthetic shantungs require a cooler iron setting than silk shantung, and seams must be spread carefully before pressing since narrow, pressed-in creases along the seamline are nearly impossible to remove); —doesn't ravel excessively, so it needs only simple seam finishes (if the garment will be lined, trimming is all that is required; if unlined, you can hand overcast the edges or finish them with a narrow zigzag stitch).

Douppioni

More exotic than shantung, douppioni, with its exciting surface appeal, has enormous charm. Its texture and lustre are so strong that a balance must be struck between using douppioni to its best advantage and not letting it, in combination with lace and other design elements, become overwhelming.

The silk versions of douppioni possess a wonderful iridescence, a characteristic that is heightened when two colors are woven together. Silk douppioni, however, is not quite as strong as it looks; its heavily slubbed yarns vary in weight and thickness. Of course, it's those very same slubbed yarns that give douppioni its fascinating, uneven texture.

Douppioni often serves as a base for embellishment—allover pearls, beadwork, patterns with metallic threads. For specific information about embellished fabrics see "Fabrics with Embellishments" on page 27.

Douppioni…has a highly-textured surface that hides stitches well; —has a less-than-consistent texture that can be evened out with underlining, such as a lightweight organza or batiste in a skirt or a medium-weight poly-cotton batiste in high-stress areas of a bodice; —tends to allow an underlying fabric to show through and affect the color of the douppioni (for example, a less-than-white douppioni will look whiter with a bright white underlining or appear creamier with an off-white one); —is easy to handle and stitch and requires no special seam finishes or hem treatments; —is easy to piece horizontally, because seams practically disappear and bias strips (cut on the bias but pieced on the straight of grain) can be lengthened imperceptibly simply by piecing horizontal edges together; —can flatten out if overpressed, causing it to lose its texture (seam allowances must be meticulously spread apart before pressing; narrow pressed-in creases will be nearly impossible to remove); —tends to show seam allowances after pressing; use narrow paper strips under seams when pressing to eliminate the problem, and press lightly).

Brocade and Damask

Regal-looking in a gown (and all too often overlooked as a fabrication possibility), brocade and damask convey a magnificent beauty through the depth and intricacy of their designs. Both fabrics are woven on special looms, called jacquard looms, that allow for very detailed designs—often floral—with raised patterns and contrasting surfaces. Metallic threads are often used, as are multiple colors.

Brocade and damask…are usually fairly heavy (brocade even more so than damask), making silk organza often the perfect underlining (for sturdier support, cotton organza or even net works well); —are usually cooperative to sew; —will dull scissors if the fabric has metallic threads; —require careful layout, such as placing and matching prominent design features precisely and avoiding flipping pattern pieces when cutting and garment pieces when joining, because subtle differences in the right side and the wrong side can be unexpectedly prominent if mismatched; —should be pressed at low temperatures if the fabric contains metallic threads; —can have hand-overcast or machine-zigzag-stitched seam allowances or, if the garment will be lined, simply trimmed and pressed seam allowances; —responds beautifully to an enhanced hemline (incorporate horsehair to shape it, or pad it to play up the fabric's thick, rich nature).

Crepe

When it comes to flowing, elegant grace, the weighty crepes with their tightly crimped yarns are a class by themselves. Although sometimes tricky to work with, they can be tamed. The newest category of polyester microfiber crepes mimic the drape and feel of costlier silk crepes.

Crepe…can be maddeningly slippery to cut (serrated scissors are a great help); —needs to be laid out with attention to grainlines because grain is very difficult to see in crepe but hang and drape are central to this fabric's appeal; —requires sharp needles and fine pins; —requires careful matching to an underlining, which must mimic the crepe's behavior without adding too much bulk or weight (for heavier silk crepes, try crepe de chine, silk georgette, or a gauzy cotton; medium-weight crepes can be self-underlined); —puckers and slips when stitched, making it difficult to sew straight-as-an-arrow seams (try careful basting, using small stitches and a walking foot, and pulling the fabric taut to achieve smooth seams); —requires a pressing cloth when being pressed (press silk crepe on the wrong side with a dry iron) because it can easily shrink and water spot; —ravels, so seams on unlined garments should be hand overcast or bound with a Hong Kong finish and seams on lined garments should be trimmed and pressed; —lends itself a hand-picked or invisible zipper closure; —looks elegant with bound buttonholes or self-fabric bias loops; —allows stitches to show, so attach the hem to underlining or, if garment is not underlined, bind hem edges with narrow bias strips of self-fabric or matching crepe de chine.

Organza

This delicate favorite lends charm and lightness to a gown. It is a lovely combination of softness and strength, gentleness and firmness—soft yet strong, gentle yet capable. Although usually used as an underlining, it makes a delightful fashion fabric. Although available in both silk and polyester, it is silk organza that is both soft and firm. Polyester organza tends to be slippery, making it difficult to handle.

Organza…is stiffened with silk's natural gum (some of which is left in during processing); —gives garments an airy effect because it is sturdier than chiffon but less fragile than tulle; —is available in a striped form, usually a combination of organza and satin, that must be seamed carefully to ensure perfectly matched stripes; —produces spectacular shadings and color effects when layered in multiple colors; —works well with French seams; —makes lovely ruffles because it gathers well, with little bulk in the seam allowance; —can be backed with a color other than the fashion fabric color; —is often available with an embroidered border that may be wide enough to accommodate an ankle-length skirt (pieces of the border or a coordinating narrow border can then be used elsewhere in the gown; to create a long train, the border usually must be removed and reshaped to follow the curve of the hem); —can be hemmed with a traditional narrow hem, or a bias strip of silk taffeta or charmeuse (for a clean, tidy finish, use a narrow machine-stitched hem).

Taffeta

Soft and light, with a characteristic rustle, taffeta can achieve great fullness and shape without excessive weight and bulk. Sometimes considered a temperamental fabric, taffeta is tightly woven and ribbed. The ribs are created by cross, or weft, yarns that are heavier than its warp yarns. These ribs are so tightly woven that they are difficult to detect. This contrasts with fabrics such as moiré and faille (a fabric similar to moiré but without moiré's distinctive water marks), where the ribs are much more prominent. Taffeta is sometimes used as a base for embellishment, either as a border or as a full-width fabric. For more information on embellished fabrics, see "Fabrics with Embellishments" on page 27.

Taffeta…derives its characteristic rustle, or scroop, from the fabric's tight weave; —is prone to water spots; —may need a nap layout, depending on its sheen; —puckers when stitched on the straight of grain (try redrawing seams to be slightly off grain; basting, adjusting stitch size, pulling the fabric taut as it is sewn, and firm pressing after stitching can also help minimize puckers); —requires a skirt underlining that will maintain taffeta's light, bouffant quality, such as silk organza (use a heavier underlining, such as cotton batiste or even lightweight flannel for bodices if boning channels need to be camouflaged); —doesn't ease well but gathers beautifully (a small gathering stitch is difficult to pull, however, because the stitches get stuck in taffeta's tightly-woven fibers); —marks easily but retains tiny holes and other marks from pins, needles, and tracing wheels; —requires fine dressmaker pins for pinning through multiple layers of the fabric's tight weave; —snags easily, so should be sewn only with a small, brand-new sewing machine needle; —has a tendency to crease along seamlines if the seams aren't completely spread open before pressing; —ravels, so seam allowances in unlined pieces should be hand overcast or finished with a narrow zigzag; —should be hemmed by stitching to an underlining because hemming stitches will show; —looks elegant with a reasonably deep hem (there is no bulk to worry about) that gives weight to the bottom of the skirt.

Moiré

A quietly elegant fabric with a surface interest that doesn't overpower gowns and evening wear, moiré is ribbed and has a water-marked appearance (moiré is the French word for watered). Engraved rollers press the design into the fabric; chemicals or heat may or may not be applied to make the finish permanent. An easy fabric to sew, moiré is available in a wide range of colors, from the subtle to the vibrant. The home furnishings department of fabric stores carry this reasonably priced fabric, which is often overlooked as a couture fabric. Moiré is sometimes found in silk, but is more commonly found in polyester.

Moiré…is best stored on a cardboard tube because creases in it are difficult to remove; —needs a nap layout; —has delicate fibers that a tracing wheel will cut; —works best with soft, light underlinings, such as silk organza or cotton batiste; —has a tendency to show ripped-out seams, making careful basting and fitting essential before stitching; —gathers and pleats beautifully, especially with the right underlining to hold the folds and puffs gently aloft; —ravels, so seams in unlined pieces should be hand overcast or finished with a zigzag stitch, and seams in lined pieces should be carefully trimmed and pressed; —hides small hand stitches well, which allows it to be hemmed to itself or to an underlining.

Tulle

Nothing replicates the airy, ballerina-like look and feel of a full, multi-layered tulle skirt. Tulle is delicate, but its fragile nature is what makes it so appealing. Although pure silk tulle is available, it's costly and extremely fragile, and doesn't have the loft of the more commonly used polyester version.

Tulle…snags easily and so requires careful handling, especially near chair legs, sharp edges, scissor points, or the zipper of a garment bag; —makes a lovely full skirt when used in six to eight layers over a taffeta underskirt (for a loftier look, insert one or more layers of stiff net; for a shaded look, alternate white and cream or insert a layer of another color, such as pink or peach); —comes in widths up to 108 inches, which is the perfect width for skirts; —looks best in skirts that are ankle length or have a short sweep train (long tulle trains are bulky and often unattractive when bustled); —makes a

Special Treatment for Tulle

Tulle's filmy nature makes it somewhat tricky to handle. In fact, working with it is almost like cutting, stitching, and pressing a cloud. The following are some helpful hints for handling this light fabric.

Cutting. Purchase a wide piece of tulle and you may be able to eliminate the center back seam (for a dropped waist design, for example) by cutting the skirt in a circle. Before cutting, be sure to calculate the skirt length carefully so that you can reduce the tedious work of trimming the layers later to make straight and uniform hems. Tulle is such a thin fabric that you can cut multiple layers at once. For best results, hold them in place with weights rather than pins, and use sharp scissors. Then, baste all layers together along the top edge of the skirt before moving the tulle from the cutting surface.

Stitching. Tulle is easy to stitch, but go slowly when machine stitching. Since the fabric is mostly air, threads can tangle easily and break, and camouflaging a new thread is difficult. To minimize tearing above a back opening, stabilize seam allowances with a row of stitching along the seamline on either side.

Pressing. For best results, press tulle with the highest temperature it will tolerate (experiment on scrap pieces of fabric), and be aware that polyester tulle melts easily. Tulle is tedious to press if it's badly wrinkled, so press out prominent wrinkles before cutting and try to avoid wrinkling the fabric while working on it. Seam allowances can be pressed open.

Hemming. For a lightweight, floaty look, leave hem edges untreated or apply a narrow ribbon. Sew the ribbon slowly along the top and bottom edges, stitching in the same direction both times. Be sure the ribbon is long enough to circle each layer of the skirt without piecing, which will spoil the effect.

---

perfect base for sequins, which can be glued to the topmost layer of tulle or to the second layer for a more subtle effect; —gathers beautifully (gather tulle separately from an underskirt or gather all the layers together; after gathering, leave the layers unseparated for a flatter look along the top edge or pull them apart for greater loft).

Chiffon

Ethereal chiffon—it floats and swirls like no other fabric. It looks beautiful in just about any application—ruffled, flounced, single layered in sleeves and upper bodices, and multilayered in skirts. It lends a magical touch, either subtle or bold, when colors are layered. And satin-striped chiffons (stripes of satin, and sometimes metallic threads, are interspersed with chiffon) can be multilayered to produce a cross-hatched effect. A plain weave fabric available in silk and polyester, chiffon is sheer but strong, and it drapes wonderfully, especially the higher-quality silk chiffons. Georgette is a variation of chiffon in which both lengthwise and crosswise yarns are crimped, resulting in a grainy texture.

Chiffon…is tricky to lay out because its lighter-than-air quality makes it difficult to handle (lay chiffon on top of another fabric, such as an old sheet, to help it cling to the cutting surface); —is much easier to cut if serrated scissors are used; —looks clean and elegant if seamed with French seams, or if seam allowances are hand overcast with small stitches; —doesn't need an underlining, which would counteract the very nature of chiffon, but, for modesty's sake, requires underlayers of sturdier fabrics in skirts (try taffeta or crepe de chine); —needs to hang before hemming if cut in a circle for a full skirt (remember that part of the skirt will lengthen because it has been cut on the bias); —looks lovely with any of several hem finishes, including a reasonably wide, slip-stitched hem if the skirt is cut on the straight of grain (the double layer of fabric deepens the color and firms the bottom edge); a hand-rolled hem, which is the traditional couture finish for chiffon but is easier to do in silk chiffon than polyester chiffon; and a narrow machine-sewn hem, which creates a beautifully clean finish.

Linen

Linen is cool, sophisticated, lightweight, easy to wear, and available in an array of weights, colors, weaves, cutwork patterns, and embroidered styles. Although perhaps not the first possibility that comes to mind as fabrication for a wedding gown or formal wear, linen, makes a perfect choice for many occasions—for example, an outdoor summer wedding that calls for a casually chic Audrey Hepburn–inspired style.

Linen…folds, pleats, and gathers beautifully; —brings life to details like piping, godets and slot seams; —is easy to sew and not at all temperamental; —adapts well to several seam finishes (lighter weight linens can be sewn with French seams, or their seam allowances can be hand overcast or zigzag stitched); —should be pressed with high heat on the wrong side, using a pressing cloth to eliminate scorching and glazing (linen's natural wax content makes it prone to glazing); —will not wrinkle excessively if the bodice is fitted and firmly underlined; —gathers so well that a full skirt with a circumference as large as six feet isn't overly full at the waist and has a beautiful shape and swing at the hem; —works well when full skirts are cut on the lengthwise straight-of-grain, creating only one seam (usually center back) and allowing the selvage edge to be placed along the top edge for gathering; —doesn't lend itself to trains because it doesn't flow as well as many other bridal fabrics and it bustles awkwardly; —can be hemmed inconspicuously or can be folded into a pleat along or slightly above the hemline, creating a design detail that camouflages hem stitches.

Fabrics with Embellishments

Although pearls, beads, and sequins are often applied to a net base, fashion fabrics themselves are sometimes embellished. Embellished fabrics are

Special Treatment for Embellished Fabrics

Embellished fabrics require special attention when being cut, seamed, pressed and hemmed. Here are a few tips for working with ornamented fabrics.

Cutting. Use an old pair of scissors when cutting embellished fabrics; accidently nicking some beads or sequins will quickly dull scissors' blades.

Stitching. Before sewing, clear the seam allowances of all ornamentation. Doing so will reduce bulk and make basting and stitching easier. Then, carefully line up and baste seams, especially those to be seamed to a nonornamented fabric, which will be noticeably lighter in weight. When machine stitching, go slowly, encouraging the needle to slide to the side of beads close to the seamline; that way, you'll reduce, and possibly eliminate, needle breakage. And use an adjustable zipper foot, positioned so its inner edge lines up exactly with the seamline. After stitching, examine the seamline, then fix any fashion fabric areas where too many beads were removed or have become loose. Embellished fabrics tend to be bulky along the seams, so use a catch stitch to hold the seam allowances flat against the underlining.

Pressing. Embellished fabrics don't really wrinkle much. But if pressing is necessary, apart from pressing seam allowances, place the fashion fabric face down on a thick towel and top both with a pressing cloth. Take care not to overpress and pucker the fabric, and don't let the embellishments come in contact with steam or heat; sequins will melt and pearls will lose their coatings.

Hemming. A faced hem is ideal for embellished fabrics. Its advantages include reducing the bulk of a folded hem, preventing the wearer from being scratched by ornamentation, cutting down on garment weight, and using the embellished fabric economically.

costly and, if heavily embellished, become weighty.

If you are combining an embellished fabric with another fabric, consider the embellished fabric's background color (which is usually white or off-white silk douppioni or silk taffeta). Sometimes, the colors of the fabrics must match perfectly; other times the match is less important. Whenever possible, compare the fabrics in natural light.

Embellished fabrics…are best used for simple designs with minimum of shaping since plenty of interest is provided by the fabric itself; —must be examined carefully to determine the fabric's pattern of embellishment, which may be closely or widely spaced; —can be underlined with silk organza, which adds stability without adding weight; —work well with hand-picked zipper closures.

Lace

Today, we are fortunate to have access to a large variety and quantity of lace. No longer is lace-wearing the province of aristocracy, as it was by law in the 17th and 18th centuries. No longer are French and Italian lacemakers forbidden to leave their native countries and take their craft with them, as was the case in the 17th century. No longer must lacemakers work in damp basements to keep fine flax fibers from drying out or in dimly lit rooms to keep candle soot from discoloring their work.

The development of the Leavers and Schiffli lace machines in the late 1800s revolutionized the speed with which lace could be made, thereby widening its availability and popularity. This brought to a close the tedious way of life of the European lacemakers, who at one time numbered 250,000 in France alone. Instead of producing a mere one-third inch of lace in one week, today's methods and machines can make a yard and a half of lace in one hour. Although it is sad that the craft has disappeared, the conditions under which lace was made and the time it took to produce it exacted a heavy toll on the lacemakers.

Happily, though, what has developed out of centuries of painstaking devotion is a contemporary lace industry rooted in the traditions of the past. Many laces still bear the names of the cities from which they originally came: Alençon, Chantilly, Venise, Valenciennes. Although they have lost much of their minutely fine detail, the beautiful laces of today link us to the skill and creativity of the lacemakers of the past.

While one of the costliest of fabrics, there is little or no waste when working with lace, and it can be stunning even in the smallest amounts. A quarter yard of silk satin is beautiful, but it would be difficult to make such a small piece the stylistic focus of an important dress, no matter how cleverly the fabric is used. A quarter of a yard of stunning, well-chosen and effectively placed lace, however, can transform a gown (Figure 2-1).

Fine lace abounds with contradictions. Although delicate in appearance,

Laces: **top row:** *embellished Alençon lace, ribbon lace, embroidered organza, sequined Chantilly lace, metallic Chantilly lace;* **bottom row:** *guipure lace, Schiffli lace, embellished Chantilly lace, beaded Chantilly lace, plain Alençon lace;* **in basket:** *Venise lace, Alençon lace with three-dimensional appliqués;* **on mannequin:** *Alençon lace apron over a Chantilly lace skirt. (See larger photo on the following spread.)*

Figure 2-1: There was just enough antique needlepoint lace to trim the front bodice and lower sleeves of this satin gown.

fine lace is far stronger than it looks. High-quality lace is beautifully made, evenly registered, and well finished. Although you might imagine such an exotic and fragile-looking fabric to be difficult to work with, the opposite is true. Lace is cooperative and forgiving. It can be cut and pieced endlessly as well as shaped, patched, overlapped, appliquéd, and invisibly seamed.

TYPES OF LACE

Lace is available in a variety of fibers, designs, and forms. Often woven from a combination of fibers, lace can be created from silk, cotton, nylon, polyester, rayon, and even wool. The variety of patterns, designs, feel, and effects is endless. Lace is wonderful to look at and to get to know, for it reveals its nuances to the careful observer.

There are a number of laces commonly available and in wide use in wedding gowns and evening wear. The following are some of the most popular.

Alençon Lace

Woven on Leavers machines, Alençon lace is the most popular lace for wedding gowns, and understandably so. Alençon lace is beautiful, sturdy, and available in a wide variety of

Lace Terminology

Allover. A wide lace, with straight edges on both sides, featuring an allover repetitive pattern.

Appliqués. Individual lace designs that can be purchased separately or cut from a larger piece of lace.

Bobbin Lace. One of the two main types of lace in which threads are held on spools, or bobbins, and are crossed and twisted into patterns while anchored with pins to a pillow.

Bride *(breed).* A French word for a small bar of threads that links various lace or embroidery motifs.

Cordonnet *(cor-dun-ay´).* The thread or fine cord that outlines the motifs on a piece of lace, strengthening both the motif and the lace and giving the lace a three-dimensional quality.

Flounce. A piece of lace with one scalloped edge.

Galloon. A piece of lace with two scalloped edges (Figure 2-2).

Figure 2-2: This Alençon lace galloon clearly separates itself into two mirror-image borders.

Insertion. A narrow strip of lace, often Valenciennes, that is inserted between two pieces of fabric.

Lace. From the French word lacis, which means a network of threads.

Leavers. The finest of the lacemaking machines.

Needlepoint Lace. One of the two main types of lace in which a net background is embellished (see Figure 2-1).

Raschel. A lace-making machine.

Re-Embroidered Lace. A needlepoint lace in which the motifs have been outlined with a silken cord.

Reseau *(ray-zo´).* French for "network"; the net background of a piece of lace.

Set. A variety of widths in which a particular lace design is produced.

designs and forms. Alençon lace almost always consists of floral motifs on a net background. The motifs themselves are outlined with a silken cord (hence, the lace is categorized as a re-embroidered lace), which gives the lace stability and firmness as well as a three-dimensional quality. For further visual interest, a variety of net patterns usually appears within the motifs themselves.

On fine quality Alençon laces, the cords that outline the motifs are carefully applied using hand-guided machines. Along the edges of the lace, there are a series of short threads, or whiskers, left from cutting the lace off the machine. Never trim them; cutting them off will weaken the lace, as well as destroy a traditional hallmark of fine quality Alençon lace.

Motif size within the lace is important to note, as is the density of the motifs. Alençon lace comes in a variety of widths, from $1/2$-inch to 36-inches wide. The borders on the 36-inch lace, which are always scalloped, are an important design feature and are worth evaluating as to width, depth, and beauty of the scalloped edge and accompanying motifs.

Although available in colors, the widest variety of Alençon lace patterns is found in white and off-white. Some are plain, some are embellished. Embellishments typically include pearls, beads, and sequins. The pearls may be all the same size or they may vary in size, and the sequins may range in color from milky to silvery to iridescent.

Allover Lace

This is usually a domestically produced lace, available in widths up to 60 inches. Allover lace is usually lightweight with a fairly simple, repeated pattern. There are no borders, and although inexpensive and economical to use, allover lace is difficult to piece invisibly and lacks the impact necessary for use as a focal point on a bodice.

Chantilly Lace

Chantilly lace is similar to Alençon lace but without the cord re-embroidery. Chantilly lace is outlined, but very subtly; the cord used is quite fine, maintaining the lace's soft, delicate hand. This gentle lace is breathtaking, and although not found in as wide a variety as Alençon, is available in white, off-white, and colors; in 36-inch widths, and galloons. Chantilly laces may be embellished: Sometimes, they have drifts of sequins to accentuate their delicate nature, and sometimes they are woven with a combination of metallic and nonmetallic threads.

Guipure Lace

The medieval French word "guiper" means to cover with silk, and perhaps the thick look of today's guipure lace is derived from silk-covered cords. Today's guipure laces are embroidered on a foundation material that is later dissolved, leaving only the motifs.

Guipure laces have allover patterns that are usually directional. They are easy to cut apart between motifs and ravel little if the motifs themselves aren't cut. They come in a limited variety of widths, but they lend themselves to many creative uses; for example, you can easily cut off a line of motifs to form a narrow strip. They are rarely embellished, although you can decorate them later—for example, you might place a single pearl in the center of each motif. Guipure laces are often quite shiny and usually fairly heavy, an advantage in that they will shape and hold their form nicely. However, gravity will pull them downward and they will shift unless stabilized, so you may need to tack them to an underlying fabric.

Ribbon Lace

Ribbon lace is a variation of Chantilly or Alençon lace in which the lace is further enhanced by the addition of a narrow ribbon that is sewn perpendicular to the lace. The ribbon is hand or machine applied, and it outlines motifs or is shaped into flowers. Rare and exquisite, beautifully made ribbon lace is the most three-dimensional of the laces.

Schiffli Lace

Delicate floral designs are embroidered on a net background, with a chain stitch or satin stitch. This lightweight lace has a simple, delicate beauty and almost an old-fashioned look. The base fabric is English net, which is stronger than the net usually used for lace. The embroidery is sometimes done in color—dark green embroidered foliage and pastel flowers, for example. Beautiful Schiffli borders are also available.

Soutache Lace

This is a variation of Alençon lace in which the motifs are re-embroidered with a soutache cord. The outlines are bolder than those created in Alençon lace, and the cord used is sometimes a contrasting color—black cord on white lace, or red cord on black lace, for example. When used appropriately, they are wonderfully striking.

Valenciennes Lace

Sometimes called "val" laces, Valenciennes laces are narrow strips of delicate, floral-patterned lace, which are used frequently for French hand sewing and insertions.

Venise Lace

Venise laces are similar to guipure laces (in fact, the names are often used interchangeably) in that they have no net background and consist of embroidered motifs. More delicate in appearance than guipure laces, they are often quite intricate, especially along their edges. They are a wonderful choice for edgings and trims.

CHOOSING LACE

Fine lace is so intrinsically beautiful that it is often overwhelming to choose from the vast number of exquisite possibilities. Although there are some general guidelines to follow, the most important consideration for selecting lace is often the placement of the lace on the gown.

Lace Layout Considerations

To visualize the placement of lace on a gown and accurately calculate yardage,

General Guidelines for Choosing Lace

Select the Best Lace. Buy the best lace you can afford. Fine laces are cooperative, intricately designed, and interesting to look at. It is better to work with less of a fine lace than with more of an inferior version. If cost is a concern, look for laces that lend themselves well to being cut into appliqués. Well-placed appliqués can be effective as well as economical.

Consider the Lace Color. Match the colors of lace and fashion fabrics carefully. There are times when you can sacrifice a perfect color match, and times when you can't. For example, if you've selected one lace for the bodice and something similar for the skirt hem, then the distance between them will likely permit a slight variation in color. And sometimes, using the right motif is more important than matching the color perfectly. Be sure to compare your choices in natural light. Fabric stores typically use fluorescent lighting, under which colors look and combine differently from the way they do in natural light. Take your choices to a window, or even outside. If the lace has sequins, be sure they are the color you want; some are markedly colored; if you are combining laces, be sure the sequins are all of the same color.

Know the Idiosyncrasies of Certain Laces. Some laces will ruffle attractively; others will not. A Chantilly lace will form soft ruffles while Alençon lace will make firmer ones. When examining Alençon laces, check to see if there are any loose cords. Loose ends require extra work to secure, and they will continue to fray, even if gone over with thread. Re-embroidered motifs sometimes pull up the net background to which they are applied. If the tension between the re-embroidering and the net is too great, the net may be puckered and unattractive. Fortunately, this is rarely a problem on the best-made re-embroidered laces. On any lace with a net background, check for small tears in the net. One or two tears can be repaired, but more than that will be difficult to work around.

Know the Special Qualities of Ornamented or Embellished Lace. Pearls, beads, paillettes, and sequins are attached to lace by hand sewing or a chain stitch (Figure 2-3). Hand-sewn embellishments are easiest to stabilize during construction and least likely to come off during construction and wear. Embellishments applied with a chain stitch pull loose easily and, therefore, require extra care in cutting and sewing, as well as more stabilizing. Although chain-stitched pearls are a beautiful embellishment, they require a great deal of extra work. Whichever ornamentation you choose, be sure that it's securely sewn on. Rubbing your hand over the surface of the lace will tell you if the ornamentation is tight or loose.

Figure 2-3: The motifs on this Chantilly lace have been completely covered with sequins securely sewn on by hand.

always shop with a full set of muslin pattern pieces. Lay the pattern pieces under the lace so you'll have a sense of how the motifs will actually look on the finished garment (Figure 2-4).

If a wide piece of Alençon lace doesn't seem quite right for your pattern pieces, experiment with narrower widths; sometimes a 16-inch or so galloon is wide enough for a bodice. And if a small corner of a muslin pattern piece doesn't quite fit on the lace, you can easily piece it later.

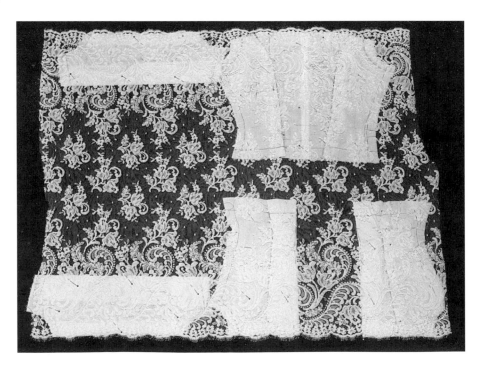

Figure 2-4: Here, muslin pattern pieces have been placed under a piece of lace. The side backs and center backs have been pinned together, and the side fronts and center front have been pinned together. Notice the borders, symmetry, and spacing and location of prominent motifs.

USING LACE BORDERS

Examine the borders of lace carefully, since they will no doubt figure into the design of the garment. Beautiful borders are one of the hallmarks of fine lace, so it makes sense to use them as fully as you can (Figure 2-5).

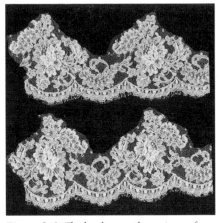

Figure 2-6: The borders on these pieces of Alençon lace are mirror images of one another.

Figure 2-5: The full, intricate borders of this lace can be used anywhere: They can cover the sleeves, with the edge of the border placed at the wrists, or they can cover much of a bodice. The inner panels can be used elsewhere—perhaps on a gown's skirt. They can be positioned as is or cut into appliqués.

The border may be taken from either a wide piece of lace or from narrow coordinating laces. If you've selected a galloon, remember that one yard of it will yield two yards of useable border lace (Figure 2-2).

On Alençon lace, you'll notice that the borders are almost always mirror images of one another, rather than exact repeats (Figure 2-6). Guipure laces are usually directional, and they often have two markedly different borders. If need be, you can sometimes create a new border within the lace.

Also consider Alençon lace sets. If you've found the perfect bodice lace, for example, but there isn't enough border to trim the sleeves, look for a matching narrow galloon. You might also consider using several different

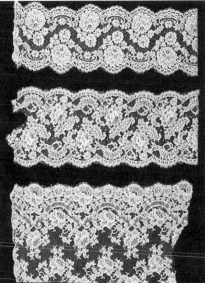

Figure 2-7: Although not a set, these different laces work well together. All three have similarly sized motifs, and the scalloped borders of the galloons are close enough in size to coordinate with one another. The top galloon, which is unembellished and, therefore, lighter in weight and less expensive, could be used to trim the skirt. The middle galloon, which is embellished, could be more prominently positioned—to trim the bodice, for example. The bottom piece of lace could be used at the base of the gown's sleeves or to fill in areas of the bodice.

laces in a gown, if they combine nicely. Although the three laces shown in Figure 2-7 are not part of a set, they work well together.

Remember, if you're planning a lace border along the top of an off-the-shoulder bodice, you'll no doubt want to coordinate that placement with the border placement at the top of the

Figure 2-8: Notice how the motifs on this guipure lace match across the top of the bodice and the sleeve. The border placement at the bottom of the bodice also mimics the border placement at the bottom of the sleeve.

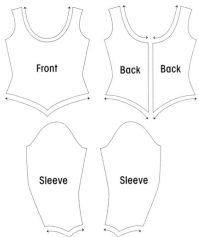

Figure 2-9: The arrows indicate typical placements of lace borders. You also may want to place lace around the skirt hem.

sleeves so that the border appears to be continuous around the entire top of the gown (Figure 2-8). When calculating the yardage, you'll need to include the neckline, base of the bodice, bottom of the sleeves, possibly even around the skirt hem (Figure 2-9).

If you are planning to use a border prominently around a V neckline in the front and back of a bodice, then the beauty and proportions of the border scallops are paramount. A petite bride, for example, will want a border and motifs scaled to her size; large motifs and wide scallops will overwhelm her. Tiny scallops and small motifs, by the same token, will be lost on a larger silhouette.

USING LACE MOTIFS

Like borders, motifs—whether large or small, intricate or fairly simple—play a vital role in a gown's appearance. Some motifs are clearly directional; others are not and look attractive in any position.

The placement of lace motifs on sleeves is generally symmetrical. To achieve this mirror image, you can place the pattern pieces on opposite sides, rather than side by side on the lace (Figure 2-10). For long sleeves, you'll want to pay careful attention to the motif in the wrist areas, which will be quite prominent in the finished gown. If the sleeves end in a V at the wrists, for example, you might look for a motif that echoes the V shapes.

When selecting lace for the bodice, be careful not to pick a piece in which you'll have to place a prominent motif

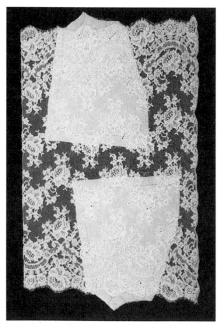

Figure 2-10: *These lower sleeve muslins have been placed under the lace. The border is so beautiful that the V in the lower edge of the sleeve may be modified to mimic the lace border. Conversely, the border itself may later be shaped to follow the original V of the sleeve.*

at the apex of the bust; a strong three-dimensional lace will direct attention to the area. If you see a particularly striking motif, imagine how wonderful it will look placed in the center of the bodice in the V of a basque-style waist.

WORKING WITH LACE

Once you've chosen a beautiful lace, your next steps are to lay out the pattern and cut and stitch the lace. Here are some things to keep in mind as you proceed; they are listed in the order in which they should be done. Working with lace is a pleasure; the effect lace produces is worth every penny and every minute spent on it.

Dyeing Lace

Lace is very easy to dye with tea, coffee, or dyes especially created for the purpose. Since many laces are a combination of fibers, some of which will dye differently from others, it is best to make samples, then carefully evaluate them in natural light. Sometimes the results are striking; for example, a darker outline on a lace motif can look dramatic. Other times, the effect isn't what you want. Testing will reveal any idiosyncrasies.

After taking the lace from the dye bath, remove excess moisture by wrapping the dyed lace in a towel. Do not wring it out—that will distribute the moisture and color unevenly. Lay the lace flat to dry; hanging it on a clothesline will allow the moisture and color to collect at the bottom of the lace, which will result in a subtle but noticeable variation in color.

Pressing Lace

Lace doesn't wrinkle the way most fabrics do, but it still needs some pressing to smooth out the net background before you lay out the pattern pieces and do any cutting; the discrepancy in tension between the plain net and the heavily embellished net often creates little puckers. Pressing with steam iron

or a damp pressing cloth will also take care of any shrinkage, which is usually minimal. When pressing laces—especially Alençon and guipure laces—you'll need to press carefully to retain their three-dimensional qualities. (Note that ribbon lace is too delicate to press.) Here are two general tips for pressing lace and achieving good results.

First, never press directly onto the right side of the lace. Doing so will flatten the motifs, and any impurities on the sole plate of the iron will be transferred to the cords of the lace (pearls will lose their coating and sequins will curl up and lose their shine). Press lace face-down on a thick terry towel and top the lace with a damp pressing cloth or use a steam iron and a dry pressing cloth. When pressing guipure lace, don't press too hard, or you will lose the lace's lovely padded quality.

Second, lace is often coated with a sizing, which gives it some stiffness, or body, and the lace will soften after repeated use and washing. Starch will temporarily restore some of the crispness, as will ironing on waxed paper. Place the lace face down on a terry towel, top with waxed paper, and use a pressing cloth.

Cutting and Trimming Lace

After determining a layout, cut out the lace pieces, leaving generous seam allowances so seams can be overlapped (Figure 2-11). Before cutting, make sure muslin pattern pieces are symmetrically lined up along any borders that will be featured in the gown. If individual motifs will be used, trim the net close to the corded outline of the motif but leave a tiny amount of net so that the threads holding the cord in place aren't weakened. Small, sharp scissors are the best tool for trimming.

Stabilizing Embellishments on Lace

When cutting and trimming lace, some of the threads holding the embellishments in place will inevitably be cut. To minimize thread cutting, study the

Figure 2-11: These bodice lace pieces have been cut out, leaving wide seam allowances for overlapping wherever necessary.

Figure 2-13: Silk organza will underline this short sleeve; although the underlining's seam allowances are wide, the lace's needn't be, as long as it reaches the stitching lines.

reverse side of the lace. Then, after cutting, stabilize the threads either by restitching the beads that are affected or by applying a tiny amount of tacky glue to the wrong side of the affected threads. You may find you need a beading needle if the holes in the beads are small; in some beads, such as tiny seed beads, the holes are minute. When gluing, be sure to let the glue dry thoroughly; a spot of it on the fashion fabric would be disastrous.

Marking Lace

Lace should be marked clearly and carefully. If you will be placing it over another fabric, you can mark that fabric, then join the two layers and treat them as one. If you must mark the lace directly, use a method called thread tracing. Here's how to do it: With a contrasting color of thread and the muslin pattern piece in place underneath the lace, baste seamlines, darts, and other important pattern marks onto the lace (Figure 2-12). Avoid using red (or a similar dark color) thread; tiny, impossible-to-remove red fibers will remain after you pull out the basting threads.

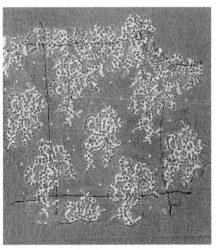

Figure 2-12: When lace is used without an underlining, stitching lines (and any other important lines) should be thread-traced.

Preparing Underlying Fabrics

Lace is often underlined (apart from being layered over a fashion fabric, as in a bodice, for example) when you want to preserve lace's transparent nature but strengthen the lace itself. Although lace is sturdy in some ways, it does have a fragile net ground that is

not always strong enough to withstand any strain. Silk organza makes an ideal underlining; it is strong, lightweight, transparent, easy to work with, affordable, and available in a wide range of colors (Figure 2-13).

Organza's natural color is the most versatile of the colors, but it does give lace a slightly milky cast; flesh-colored silk organza is more invisible against the skin. (Natural white silk organza can easily be tinted to the appropriate skin color with tea, coffee, or dye.) Different colors of underlining give different effects, of course: flesh-colored silk organza under black lace is quite different from black silk organza under black lace.

In addition to strengthening lace, an underlining provides a field for markings and tracings. Colored marks will show through silk organza, so the best way to mark white or off-white organza is with white tracing paper. Although difficult to see, the marks will be visible, and they can be gone over with hand or machine basting. After marking the organza, you can join it to the lace, following the marks on the organza.

Stitching Lace Pieces by Machine and by Hand

When stitching lace (for a fully lace-covered bodice, for example), the object is to make the lace look as if it is one continuous piece. Therefore, you will need to overlap and stitch seams as well as darts and any other shaping. Hand stitching is necessary for most laces including guipure, Chantilly, rib-

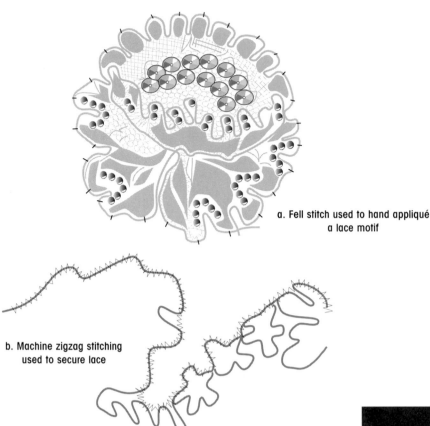

a. Fell stitch used to hand appliqué
a lace motif

b. Machine zigzag stitching
used to secure lace

Figure 2-14: Unembellished Alençon lace can be machine stitched; small zigzag stitches go back and forth over the cords. Lace can be hand stitched with a fell stitch; as with machine stitching, it secures the cords, following their outline as much as possible.

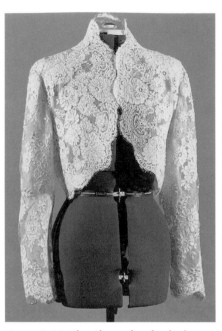

Figure 2-15: This Alençon lace border has been shaped to curve around the front edge of a bolero jacket. The lace has been cut, overlapped, and stitched onto a silk organza base.

Figure 2-16: One border has been cut and overlapped; the other has been cut and spread apart.

bon laces, and embellished laces. For hand stitching (also called hand appliquéing), use the fell stitch, an inconspicuous stitch that leaves little thread on top of the lace. It makes a secure stitch, is quick and easy to do, and allows the greatest control as you stitch and shape (Figure 2-14a). Some laces, such as unembellished Alençon, can be machine stitched, but remember that hand stitching always gives you the most stitch control and disturbs the surface of the lace the least. To machine stitch Alençon lace, use small, close zigzag stitches. Wherever possible, zigzag over the cords of the motifs so the three-dimensional nature of the lace hides the stitches (Figure 2-14b).

Shaping Lace Borders around Curves

Sometimes lace is cut and shaped independently of the fashion fabric and then layered over it. More often, however, it is stitched (and shaped) directly onto the fashion fabric, using the fashion fabric as a sturdy base on which to pin it, shape it, and secure it.

Lace borders can be cut and shaped to follow either convex or concave curves (Figure 2-15). The sharper the curves, the deeper the cuts into the lace. For a concave curve, spread the lace apart; for a convex curve, overlap the lace (Figure 2-16). If the lace will be heavily overlapped, trim some of the underlying lace to reduce bulk and clarify the motifs. If the border lace is narrow and not dramatically curved, you

may be able to eliminate cutting, and instead, shape the lace by pressing it (Figures 2-17 and 2-18).

Making Invisible Darts on Lace

Darts are easily shaped by overlapping lace. Though the original dart lines may not match perfectly, the shaping will be duplicated. When making the choice as to which side of the dart will be topmost, observe the design. The most visually pleasing motif should be topmost (although sometimes there are

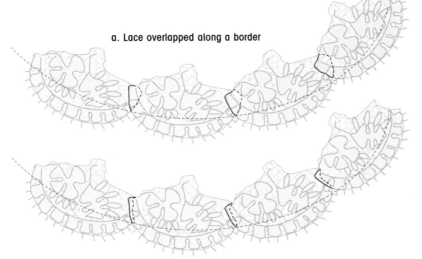

a. Lace overlapped along a border

b. Lace after it has been overlapped, stitched, and trimmed

Figure 2-17: A border is easy to shape by cutting, overlapping, stitching by hand or machine, and trimming out the excess. Follow the contour of the topmost lace when cutting out the excess underneath lace; a straight cutting line will often show through the top layer of lace.

Figure 2-18: Pressing with steam (the lace is placed right side down into a thick towel) is enough to shape these narrow borders.

Figure 2-19: This lace has been cut in preparation for a dart. The edges will be overlapped, stitched along the topmost edge, and the excess lace underneath trimmed away.

The topmost motif alternates from side to side

Figure 2-20: Notice that the prominent motif has been chosen for the top layer and that the preferred motif switches from side to side. This technique for overlapping can be used on darts and seams.

two pleasing arrangements, and sometimes neither is particularly pleasing). Remember, too, that a patch can be used if the natural configurations in the lace aren't satisfactory. After overlapping the layers to conform to the dart's shape (Figure 2-19), stitch the edge of the top layer, and trim excess underneath lace, as necessary (Figure 2-20).

Making Invisible Seams with Lace

A beautifully fitted bodice, paired with an exquisite lace, will be spoiled by bulky seams that incorporate thick lace. A far better option is to overlap the lace, stitch the top layer in place, and trim any bulk from underneath (Figure 2-21). Although it takes careful planning, cutting, stitching, and trimming, there is no substitute for beautifully constructed

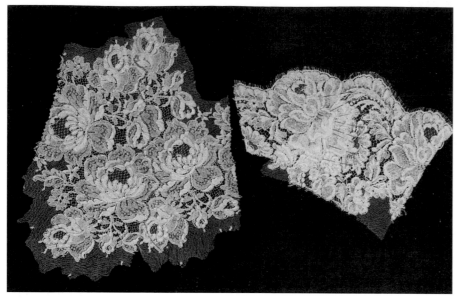

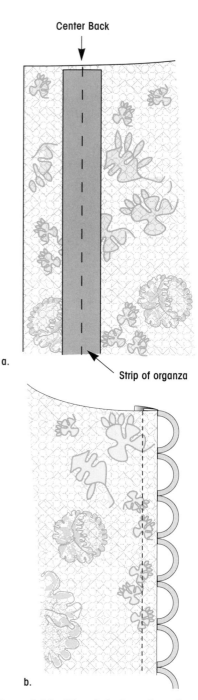

Figure 2-21: On the left, the dark zigzag stitch shows where the seam has been overlapped; the join would be imperceptible with matching thread. On the right, lace is prepared for stitching. It will look more delicate once the extra lace underneath is trimmed away.

overlapped seams. Small patches can be used to fill uncovered areas.

Finishing Lace Seam Allowances

Not all seams are overlapped. The seams on sleeves, for example, are usually trimmed after stitching, then the edges are either hand overcast or trimmed, spread open, and the edges held in place with a catch stitch. Another option is to encase the seam allowances in silk organza if it has been used as an underlining. If the organza has a wide seam allowance on one side, the extra fabric can be used to cover both seam allowances. Seam allowances can also be camouflaged; for example, seam allowances of black lace and black silk organza can be bound with organza that matches the wearer's skin tone.

Applying Closures to Lace

LOOPS AND BUTTONS

This traditional wedding gown closure is often used with lace. Sometimes the bottom half of a bodice consists of lace over a fashion fabric, while the top half is lace alone or lace over a sheer underlining. The effect is beautiful, but the upper lace must be strengthened along the back opening, and the two sides must match perfectly. Furthermore, the lace, which has some give, must lie flat without puckering, stretching, or gaping.

To add stability to a silk organza or English net underlining in the loop area, insert a narrow strip of silk organza selvage—strong but light and transparent—along the back bodice opening (Figure 2-22). Keep the strengthened seam allowance as narrow as possible to preserve the transparent nature of the gown back.

On the button side of the opening, you'll need to create a narrow placket to form an underlap, or the back will gape whenever strain is put on the opening. To strengthen the area, insert a strip of silk organza or a narrow piece of ribbon, which will be camouflaged by the buttons themselves (Figure 2-23). Then, sew the buttons just to the right of the center back so placket extends slightly to the left of the center. Be sure

Figure 2-22: Although the loops themselves will strengthen the back edge of the bodice somewhat, apply a narrow strip of silk organza before sewing them in place to guarantee a well-behaved placket with no stretching or pulling (a). Flesh-colored silk organza is practically invisible.

to hide the threads connecting the buttons in the fabric layers.

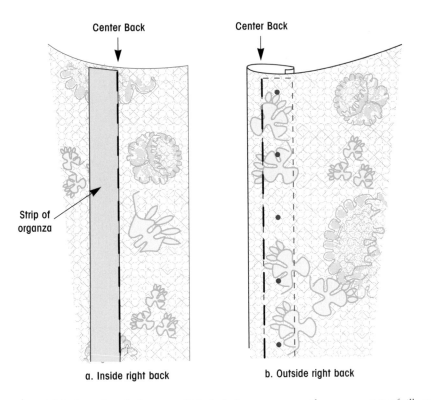

Center Back

Strip of organza

a. Inside right back

Center Back

b. Outside right back

Figure 2-23: Strengthen the base on which the buttons are sewn with a narrow strip of silk organza selvage or piece of ribbon placed along the center back line.

ZIPPERS

A hand-picked zipper makes a wonderful closure for lace; the zipper is strong, flat, and the pull on the gown is evenly distributed. Hand-picked zippers are easy to apply (Figure 2-24). The lace should extend into the seam allowance, unless individual motifs or a border that runs along the seamline are being used.

Before applying the zipper, baste the lace to the underlayer twice: once exactly along the seamline and second at the edge of the seam allowance (Figure 2-25). Remove pearls and thick embellishments from the seam allow-ance; sequins and small beads usually don't present a problem. Next, fold the seam allowance along the seamline, and prick stitch the zipper in place.

SNAPS AND HOOKS AND EYES

Snaps and hooks and eyes are useful fasteners on lace, and they are easy to apply. Unless snaps are tiny, cover them with matching silk. Place hooks with care; they will easily catch on the lace. Cover hooks and eyes with a blanket stitch if they are visible, and consider using thread bars instead of metal eyes.

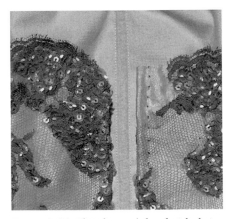

Figure 2-24: This closure (a hand-picked zipper) is nearly finished. Only a small piece of lace needs to be pieced onto the upper right near the top of the zipper.

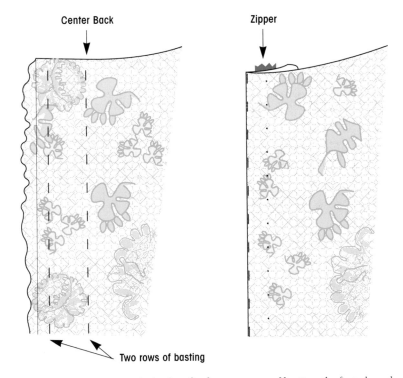

Center Back

Zipper

Two rows of basting

Figure 2-25: Lace on a zipper placket benefits from two rows of basting: the first along the fold line, the second along the outer edge of the seam allowance. Basting helps prevent the lace from sagging or being pulled out of shape at the zipper opening where it could get caught in the zipper. If unobtrusive, the basting can remain in place after the zipper has been hand picked.

PLACING LACE

Wherever you've decided to use lace—whether on the bodice, sleeves, or hem—the following design and construction hints will help you achieve the desired effect.

Lace on a Sheer Yoke

Lace used on a sheer yoke is almost always underlined to add strength and stability. On some gowns, only the top edge, which gets the most strain, is underlined. Another area that often needs strengthening is the armscye. When only a stabilizing piece of underlining is necessary, use a silk organza band, which can be positioned and fin-ished inconspicuously (Figure 2-26). Another transparent fabric that serves as a good underlining for lace is English net, which, though not as strong as silk organza, does have more give. Cut the underlining so it mimics the contour of the lace's scalloped edge. Or cut it straight across, staystitch it, turn under the seam allowance, and join it to the lace with a fell stitch or a slip stitch.

Lace on Sleeves

A sheer underlining (for example, silk organza) is used with transparent lace sleeves for several reasons: to support the weight of a heavy lace, to provide a base for appliqués or for lace that partially covers the sleeves, to make a firm base for closures and the lower edges, and to guard against tearing at the elbows or armscye areas of tight sleeves. When working with lace on sleeves, mark the underlining and baste the two layers together; from then on, treat them as one. If you remove orna-mentation from the seam allowances, you can sew the sleeve seams on the machine with a zipper foot.

Lace Borders on a Bodice

Lace borders can be used on a bodice, either around the neckline or along the base. You can cut lace borders from a wide piece of lace, purchase them separately, or create them from a galloon (Figures 2-27).

Borders sometimes appear as if they extend naturally from the lace to which they are attached, and other times, they are look entirely independent. If the borders are to look as if they extend from the lace already on an area, then carefully match the designs, keep dou-ble layers to a minimum, and arrange the lace in such a way that the behold-er's eye doesn't notice the placement. If a border is to look superimposed, determine the best placement design-wise. Then, securely stitch the lace both along the scalloped edge (slip stitch to the edge of the bodice) and along the inner edge (carefully fell stitch to the bodice).

Generally, the scallops on borders should be placed so that the apex of the scallop aligns with the edge of the base fabric. If the border is placed too much toward the body of the gown, the base fabric will show and lessen the effec-tiveness of the scallop. If it is placed too far from the body of the gown, too much of the scallop will be unbacked and, therefore, unstable (Figure 2-28).

Borders on off-the-shoulders gowns usually look best if they appear to con-tinue around the shoulders. Cut guipure lace borders from the edge of the fabric or create them from inner rows of motifs. Then, place the border neither too far into the fashion fabric, where the beauty of its outer edge will be lost, nor too far away from the fashion fabric,

Figure 2-26: A strip of silk organza or English net can strengthen a piece of bodice lace that isn't underlined. Cut silk organza on the bias if some movement is desired; otherwise cut it on the straight-of-grain. Stitch it into place loosely and inconspicuously; flesh-colored organza will practi-cally disappear once placed against the skin.

Figure 2-27: A lace galloon before being cut apart.

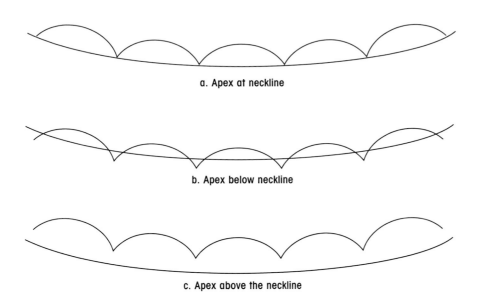

a. Apex at neckline

b. Apex below neckline

c. Apex above the neckline

Figure 2-28: Align the apex of a scalloped border with the edge of the base fabric. If the apex is too low, the underlying fabric will be visible and the effect of the scallops will be diminished; if it is too high, too much of the lace will be unsupported.

Apex at hemline

Figure 2-29: Line up the apex of a border lace along the hemline. Don't let the lace shift upward when stitching; otherwise, the effect of the scallops will be diminished.

Using a small zigzag stitch, machine stitch the lace in place through both the fashion fabric and the underlining, taking care not to distort any of the layers. Be sure the lace doesn't shift away from the hemline. If you prefer, you can stitch the lace by hand. For most laces at the hemline, one row of stitching is enough (the weight of the lace will keep it in place), but on a wide border, stitching twice—once along the top edge of the lace and once to join the lace to the fashion fabric at the hemline—will help stabilize the lace. Sew the lining, if there is one, in place after stitching the lace.

Overhanging Lace

A lace overhang is common where the bodice and skirt join (Figure 2-30). Not only does it serve to camouflage unruly gathers, but it gives a chance for a beautiful border to show. In the back of the gown, it provides a hiding place for bustling buttons or hardware to secure a detachable train. The overhang can be part of the original lace, or it can be a border that is added later. And it can appear to be a natural extension of the bodice lace, or it can be an entirely separate element. It needn't be stitched along its bottom edge—it usually overhangs a full skirt—but it can be loosely tacked at the actual seamline to help it stay in place.

where it will be unstable. Experiment until you find the best placement.

Lace Borders on a Hem

When a border is used around a gown's hem, it should be attached after hemming is complete. If you're cutting the border from a galloon, piece it as necessary. If it is a mirror-image galloon, choose a center point, which will line up with the center front of the skirt and from which the galloon will proceed symmetrically. Then line up the border's apex at the hemline (Figure 2-29), and pin the lace in place along its top edge, pinning frequently. Shape the lace by pressing if the skirt has a gentle curve; cut and overlap the lace if the curve is severe.

Figure 2-30: This guipure lace will overhang the skirt–bodice seam. Fold it out of the way when basting and stitching.

Lace Medallions

Lace medallions are favorite additions to skirts and the upper half of full sleeves. They provide an effective way of highlighting a beautiful lace pattern and bringing attention to a design feature—without using an enormous amount of lace.

Trim and position medallions carefully and attach them with a fell stitch. Then trim the fashion fabric behind the medallions to create a window effect if desired (Figure 2-31). Where the fashion fabric has been cut away, sparingly and carefully apply a seam stabilizer to the narrow fabric edges; if too much stabilizer is used, it will leech through and be seen.

The symmetrical nature of Alençon lace lends itself beautifully to cutting, reshaping, and building up large, mirror-image medallions. When carefully placed, they can be wonderfully effective—forming a triangle at the center front of the skirt, matching it to a larger one at the center back or at the base of the train, highlighting the area of the skirt that will be showcased once the gown is bustled.

Apply medallions by machine as long as there are no pearls or other embellishments to get in the way; otherwise, stitch them by hand. There is never any strain on medallions, so careful hand stitching is perfectly secure.

THREE COMMON LACE TREATMENTS

Shaping with a Single Piece of Lace

Sometimes, a single piece of lace can be wrapped around the garment, conforming to its shape (Figure 2-32). There are, however, a number of parameters if this approach is to work: the lace must be flexible and the design must be fairly straightforward (a straight skirt, a mini-dress, or a bodice for a less-than-full figure). Further, there must a piece of lace large enough to work, and the motifs within the lace must fall in the desired configuration.

First, anchor the lace around the widest part of the wearer's body; on a dress, for example, it would be anchored around the hipline, the bottom edge of the piece of lace lining up as desired. (If the bottom edge of the lace is a scalloped border, align the border along the hem of the dress.) Next, placing pins on motifs (not on the delicate net background of the lace), pin the lace downward from the hipline, making sure the hem lines

Figure 2-32: *This wide piece of lace has been anchored at the hips and hem of the underdress, then shaped upward.*

up exactly with a border, if there is one. Then pin upward from the hipline, shaping the lace as necessary.

Shaping is usually done with tucks or small darts, wherever necessary. There may be few or many tucks. Some areas may require little shaping; other areas may require extensive shaping. Tucks, darts, and overlaps will be least visible if they are hidden behind motifs rather than placed in the exposed portions of net.

After pinning the lace securely to the underlayer, hand stitch it in place. Frequent tacking, especially with heavy laces, will hold the lace in place and prevent shifting, hanging, or strain. Be careful that your stitches aren't too tight; it is easy to pull the thread a little too firmly and inadvertently tighten up entire sections. Treat tucks as you would overlapped darts: Cut the leading edge and overlap the excess. If the overlap is small, then the underlying material needn't be removed; if the overlap is large, remove the excess lace before stitching the top layer (see also pages 38–39).

Covering a Bodice with Three Pieces of Lace

Many bodices consist of seven pieces: a center front, two side fronts, two side backs, and two center backs. Thus, you could cut seven pieces of lace, and overlap and seam each seam invisibly. There is, however, a short cut.

In most cases, you can eliminate separate side back and side front lace seams.

Figure 2-31: *These lace medallions were cut from a larger piece of lace. Notice how the fashion fabric has been cut from behind the medallion on the right.*

One piece of lace can be cut for the front, and one piece can be cut for each side of the back. This is possible because lace itself is flexible, and most of the bodice shaping is done at the side seams, which will be overlapped and carefully shaped. Moreover, the back is fairly flat, except for any flare at the hip, so in almost every instance, each half of the back can be covered with a single piece of lace. In the front, where a bodice has princess seams, much of the shaping is above the apex of the bust. Again, a single piece of lace can cover the entire front, shaping it as necessary to accommodate bust curves and the flare below the waist, which is minimal in the front.

This approach has several advantages. The two back pieces can be lined up side by side for careful coordination of motifs. Further, each section is large enough so that the patterns within the lace can be clearly seen and spacing and placement can be evaluated.

To prepare for cutting the lace, first pin or baste the muslin together to make three sections: a front section and two back sections. After basting, overlap and flatten out the hip flare of the back sections; you will deal with the flare later (Figure 2-33). If the bust curve is minimal, then pin or baste the front sections together, smoothing any flare below the waist (Figure 2-34). If the bust curve is moderate or substantial, then leave the seam open above the apex of the bust (Figure 2-35). Any

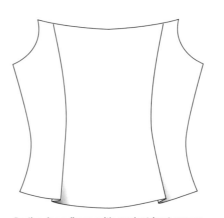

Bodice for a figure with modest bust curves

Figure 2-34: For a figure with modest bust curves, baste the three pieces of the bodice front together, overlapping the lower edge. Lace shaping is minimal. Sew the pieces together; the lace will be stretched to accommodate bust curves. Later, overlap excess lace in the armscye area as you would a dart.

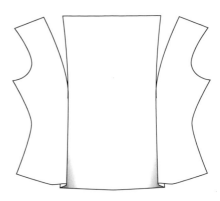

Bodice for a full figure

Figure 2-35: For a figure with considerable bust fullness, leave the muslin unstitched from the apex of the bust upward. Baste the three pieces of the bodice front together, overlapping the lower edge. Later, overlap the excess lace at the top of the bodice as you would a dart.

Figure 2-36: Guipure lace is placed on the bodice pieces: one piece covers the right back (another, placed identically, will cover the left back), and a large piece covers the front.

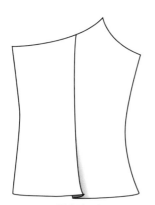

Right back

Figure 2-33: Baste the two pieces of the muslin back together, and overlap the lower edge where the hip flares, to flatten out the shaping. The flare will be dealt with after the lace is cut.

excess lace will be dealt with later (it will be treated as a dart: overlapped with the excess underlayer of lace removed). Use wide lace seam allowances wherever possible so there is plenty of lace for overlapping at the side seams. If there is a shortage of lace at the side seams, small pieces can camouflage uncovered areas.

Remember to consider motif position and direction, border placement, and symmetry of pattern when placing these bodice sections on the lace. If the gown has sleeves, then they obviously have to be worked into the layout, but their placement is usually very straight-

forward (no curves, no piecing—just a symmetrical treatment and attention to attractive motif placement in the wrist area and along the top edge, especially for off-the-shoulder gowns).

Cut the bodice lace pieces, leaving generous seam allowances on at least one side of each seam: one left side seam, either the back or front piece (best bet: both, when possible) must be able to overlap; one right side seam, either the back or front piece (best bet: both, when possible) must be able to overlap (Figure 2-36) Stitch sleeves in the usual manner; their seam allowances needn't be overly wide.

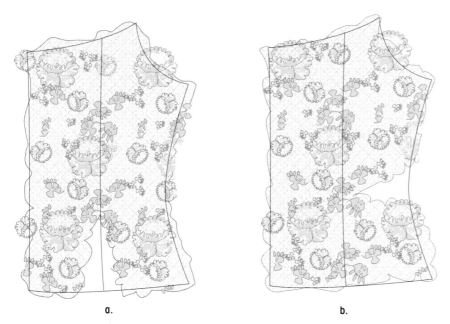

a.   b.

Figure 2-37: After joining the back bodice pieces, refine the placement and shaping of the lace. To accommodate the hip curve, split the lace from the bodice base (a) or side (b) as far as necessary toward the waist. A separate piece of lace (cut from the extra lace and carefully matched) will camouflage the split. Sometimes a side split will be camouflaged when the side seam is overlapped.

After cutting the lace for the bodice, set it aside and prepare the bodice as follows: Sew the side front seams and side back seams in the fashion fabric, then catch stitch their seam allowances. Staystitch the seamlines at the top of the bodice pieces, turn them in and catch stitch them in place. You can now attach the lace. Pin and shape the back pieces, splitting the lace to accommodate the hip flare (Figure 2-37). Note that if the flare is minimal and the lace is fairly flexible, you may be able to shape the lace without cutting it. An alternate way to handle the flare is to shift it to the side waist area and to manipulate it as you would a dart. A side split can often be camouflaged with lace that overlaps the side seam.

Pin the large piece of lace to the front of the bodice, tacking it frequently and shaping it as necessary. There may be excess lace above the apex of the bust or in the armscye area; overlap and remove the excess as you would a dart, then stitch it in place. Tack the lace close to but not up to the side seams (Figure 2-38).

Once the internal shaping has been taken care of, and the lace has been securely tacked in place, join the side

Figure 2-38: Here, guipure lace has been tacked to the fashion fabric and its underlining. Although barely visible in this photo, each motif has been tacked, avoiding the boning channels and stopping short of the side seams and the base of the bodice.

seams of the fashion fabric, and overlap and appliqué the lace in place. When overlapping the side seams, be certain that the most pleasing motifs are on top. Sometimes the back lace is on top, sometimes the front lace is on top;

more typically, it changes along the seam (see Figure 2-20). Finally, make little nips and tucks, as necessary, to perfect the lace shaping within the body of the lace.

Using Lace Appliqués

One of the charms of fine lace is that it lends itself so well to reshaping that the nature of the lace can change entirely. Appliqués are a beautiful way to use lace's flexibility.

Motifs for appliquéing can be purchased individually or easily created. The use of appliqués, which can vary in size from large sections of lace to tiny individual motifs, is the lace treatment that allows for the greatest flexibility. Pieces of lace can literally be placed anywhere and everywhere. However, this approach can involve a lot of hand work, as each piece of lace must be applied separately.

Appliqués can be used sparingly: a few motifs on the bodice or perhaps something at a basque waist and at the base of the sleeves (Figure 2-39). If you use few lace appliqués, the fashion fabric will get more attention, as will seams or other details. Appliqués can also be used in a very dense pattern (Figure 2-40). Be careful, though, not to let the

Figure 2-39: Motifs have been used sparingly on this bodice to highlight its shaping.

pattern become too intense; otherwise the overall pattern as well as the initial charm and delicacy of the lace will be lost. A dense motif can be spectacular, as long as it remains defined. When applying appliqués, remember that they can overlap and they can be applied in regular, irregular, and free forms.

In addition to being decorative, appliqués can be functional. They can cover bustling buttons at the base of a bodice, and they can camouflage bustling loops on a long skirt. Appliqués can even be applied to lace. For example, individual flower motifs can be carefully cut out, embellished with tiny glass beads, and reapplied to Alençon lace. Also, a very thin wire can be stitched around the perimeter of the back of an appliqué so that it can be shaped and become truly three-dimensional.

Figure 2-40: Although the lace on this bodice appears to be a single piece, in reality, it is many motifs that have been cut and repositioned symmetrically to highlight the intricate patterns of a particularly heavily pearled Alençon lace.

CONSTRUCTION

3

"The mood happens on the runway. The rest happens in the atelier: Couture is an inside story."

—Karl Lagerfeld

The Muslin

Preparation of a muslin pattern is the essential first step for any couture project, and it is especially crucial for a project as complex as a wedding gown. For most gowns, a muslin of the entire gown is ideal; for a sheath, it is absolutely necessary. For a traditional full-skirted gown, at least the bodice and sleeves should be made up in order to assess fit, proportion, stylistic details, and movement.

The muslin copy of the garment will become your laboratory. It will allow you to make adjustments, readjustments, and mistakes on something other than the fashion fabric, and you will be able to see where changes are needed. After it has been fitted (often more than once), it will become your pattern—accurate, durable (it won't tear), and full of invaluable information.

THE IMPORTANCE OF THE MUSLIN

A muslin, or muslin pattern, or toile (pronounced *twal*), is a copy of your garment in a fabric other than the fashion fabric. The fabric generally used for a muslin is unbleached muslin, because it's readily available, it's inexpensive, and its bland appearance makes it a good background for evaluating your work. Muslin is available in a variety of weights, so try to choose muslin of a weight similar to that of your gown's fabric. That way, it will more closely mimic the drape and behavior of the fashion fabric.

A muslin is basically a test garment, and in working with it, you have an opportunity to fine-tune fit, to add or modify design details, and to adjust proportions. It provides a chance to try challenging or unfamiliar sewing techniques and design elements, to test underlinings and boning placement, and in general, to begin to "feel at home" with a project.

The muslin can be pinned (without fear of damaging delicate fabrics), and it

can be taken apart and restitched (without fear of leaving impossible-to-remove stitching lines). It will allow you the chance to train your eye as you look at the wearer in it and allow you to experiment with all the details that add up to a successful gown: the shape and depth of

the neckline, the fullness of the sleeves, the depth and angle of the V at the base of the bodice, the width of the shoulder seams. Once the muslin has been fitted and adjusted, it is re-marked and taken apart, and you're left with a full set of pattern pieces, clearly and accurately marked. These sturdy fabric pattern pieces will be used for cutting, marking, and fitting the fashion fabric, underlining, and lining. They will be your road map when you move on to working with the actual gown fabrics.

MUSLIN CONSTRUCTION

After a design or pattern has been chosen, the client must be measured, and her measurements compared with those of the pattern. Then the pattern stitching lines must be adjusted accordingly.

Prepare the Paper Pattern

Although the fit will be fine-tuned once the muslin is actually on the wearer, certain adjustments should be made on the paper pattern. Couture garment construction does not use the standard 5/8-inch seam allowance, so stitching lines themselves must be drawn on the paper pattern if they are not already printed there (today's multisized patterns rarely contain stitching lines). A seam allowance of at least one inch (and perhaps more at the center back, shoulders, neckline, and bottom edge of the bodice) should be used. Most couture garments don't use separate facings (folded-back wide seam allowances are usually used instead), so don't bother incorporating them.

Prepare the Muslin Fabric

Properly aligned grain is one of your biggest allies, so you should straighten the grain before you do anything else. Most muslin is off grain horizontally (Figure 3-1), and a single piece of fabric may have some areas that are more off grain than others, so check carefully. To straighten the grain of fabric, pull it on the diagonal. You can true it up on a grain board or by using an L- or T-shaped ruler or the corner of a table.

Once the grain is straight, press the muslin, fold it in half lengthwise, and lay out the pattern pieces, giving your-

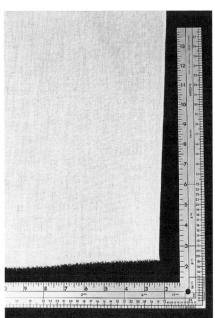

Figure 3-1: This piece of muslin is off grain; it should be straightened before being pressed and laid out.

self generous seam allowances. Remember, the muslin is for experimentation, so you want plenty of extra fabric if you decide to raise a neckline, lower a waistline, make a sleeve head puffier, or make a sleeve longer.

Mark the Fabric and Assemble the Muslin

After the muslin pieces have been cut out, the muslin fabric is ready for marking. Use old-fashioned waxed tracing paper and a tracing wheel, and stand up while marking the pieces. Standing helps you mark long straight lines smoothly and accurately.

Muslin pattern pieces should contain the following information: grainlines, center front and center back, stitching lines, dart placement, neckline, waistline, apex of the bust, match points, armholes, hemlines, the line at which the bodice attaches to the skirt, and placement of boning. In addition, each pattern piece should be labeled with its name, as well as the name or initials of the client.

With two layers of muslin pinned together and the tissue pattern on top, mark each side separately to ensure accuracy. First, place the tracing paper

on a flat surface and place the two layers of fabric on top of it, with the pinned tissue pattern facing up. Using the tracing wheel on the tissue pattern, transfer all markings to the bottom layer of muslin (Figure 3-2). Remove the paper pattern, but immediately return each pin to the muslin, keeping the layers together exactly as they were. Flip the two layers and mark the second side, using the marks you've just made as your guide (Figure 3-3). Both sides are now

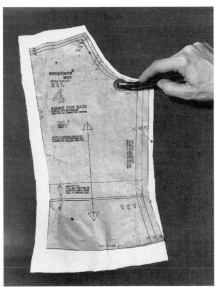

Figure 3-2: The bottom layer of the muslin is being marked; the tracing wheel will transfer the markings from the large piece of tracing paper on which the muslin rests.

Figure 3-3: The paper pattern has been removed, the pieces of muslin flipped, and the first set of marks serves as a guide for marking the second. The paper pattern is no longer needed.

marked, without any shifting of layers; sandwiching a folded piece of tracing paper between with fabric layers almost guarantees shifting and inaccuracy.

Now, on each piece, machine (or hand) baste each mark with dark-colored thread. Separately stitch each stitching line. Don't turn the corner and continue; instead, break the thread and start again. Turning the corner causes the fabric to bubble. Besides, the seamlines should extend beyond the point at which they cross, to the end of the piece of muslin. When stitching a dart, you should have three separate stitching lines—one for each leg and one for the center fold line. It isn't necessary to thread-trace match points, although any marks critical to the placement of design elements should be marked.

You can now assemble the muslin, using a hand basting stitch or a long machine basting stitch. For clarity, use a dark-colored thread, but make sure it's a different color from the basting thread.

Next, clip curved seams, and press the muslin for the first fitting. Be sure to clip and turn in the neckline seam allowance. Be careful not to stretch the neckline seam out of shape; you will stabilize it with twill tape during the fitting.

Add the Bones and Waistline Stay

After the muslin is assembled, bones and a waistline stay can be added. Boning and the waistline stay are important engineering tools; they work because the female body widens both above and below the waistline. Most gowns have a tightly fitted bodice—with or without sleeves, on or off the shoulders—and a full, heavy skirt. We've all seen a sagging bodice, the problem compounded by a heavy skirt pulling the whole gown downward. Boning and waist stays work together to counteract the force of gravity in such situations.

BONING APPLICATION

Although used primarily in strapless and off-the-shoulder gowns, boning can be useful in most fitted bodices. Bones, which used to be made of whalebone,

are narrow pieces of metal or plastic of varying lengths. Spiral steel boning, which is very lightweight despite its name, can be shaped laterally as well as bent forward and back. It is sold in numerous lengths, as well as in long pieces that can be cut to any length (although with some difficulty). Plastic boning is easily cut to desired lengths.

Bones are inserted into narrow fabric or ribbon channels that are machine basted to the muslin and later removed and re-attached to the underlining inside the gown. Fabric channels are sometimes sold with the bones. When they aren't, you can easily make them with lightweight cotton or ribbon. The bones should rest snugly inside the channels. If the channels are too tight, the bones will have a tendency to stand up on their sides; if the channels are too loose, the bones will shift rather than stay in place. Allow a little extra length so that the channels can be accurately cut to size when they're being applied. When basting the channels to the muslin, be sure to leave the bottom end of each channel open for inserting the bones (Figure 3-4).

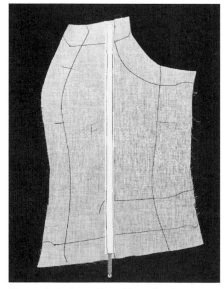

Figure 3-4: A spiral steel bone has been partially inserted into the vertical boning channel on this muslin pattern piece.

For best results, you'll probably want to use boning in several locations beyond those customarily suggested by the pattern directions. The security that

boning gives far outweighs its presence (it is, in fact, undetectable when worn, if placed properly). Experimenting with boning placement is part of the fitting process.

Typical boning placements for both off-the-shoulder and strapless bodices are shown in Figures 3-5 and 3-6, respectively. You can see the internal structure and support that both of the bodices have. Both would stay put,

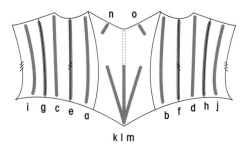

Figure 3-5: This off-the-shoulder bodice has 15 pieces of boning, not at all excessive for a well-constructed garment. Think of this gown as "hanging" from the highest points of the bodice (a, b, c, and d), almost like a suspension bridge. Other bones help smooth out the side seams (e and f), support and smooth out the bodice back (g and h), further support the back and highlight its curve (i and j). Bones k, l, and m ensure that a pointed Basque (or V) waist will stay pointed, while bones n and o counteract any pulling across the top bodice edge. Notice that no boning has been placed directly over the bust, where it can give an unnatural stiffness and leave a visible ridge. Some full bustlines, though, may require boning in this area.

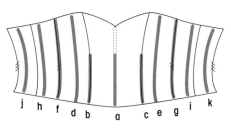

Figure 3-6: This strapless bodice uses 11 bones. Depending on the design, fullness of the bust, and fabrication, boning may be placed at the center front of the bodice, ending either at the top or part-way up (a); under the bust, up to the point at which the fullness starts (b and c); alongside the fullness of the bust (d and e); along the side seams for a smooth line (f and g); and along the back for support, smoothness, and to accentuate the curve of the back (h, i, j, and k).

show off the gown and wearer to best advantage, and add to the wearer's comfort. For more information on boning placement, see the box on page 59.

Experiment with boning during the muslin fittings, and don't be afraid to place it where you may not have considered placing it before. Remember, boning is your tool to counteract certain natural tendencies of the gown. If the bodice wants to droop, straighten it up (Figure 3-7); if it is wants to pull, pull it in the opposite direction with boning (Figure 3-8). As you work with boning, you will become more familiar with it as a tool, realizing what a valuable ally it is.

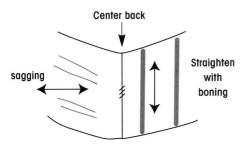

Figure 3-7: If the bodice wants to sag, counteract the sagging with boning.

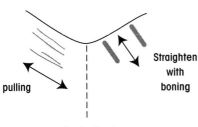

Figure 3-8: If the front wants to pull along the edges of the V, counteract the pulling with boning.

WAISTLINE STAY APPLICATION

A grosgrain waistline stay is the second half of the engineering equation. It is an anchor that works because it really can't be pulled far off center (which is the waist). Because of the female shape, which widens both above and below the waist, the waistline stay can't go up, and it can't go down. Thus, the waistline stay anchors both the bodice and the skirt—the boned bodice stands on the stay, and the skirt hangs from the stay.

Your first step in placing the waistline stay is to locate the gown wearer's natural waistline. To do this, tie a narrow piece of elastic somewhat snugly around her waist. Ask the wearer to bend forward and backward, and from side to side. The elastic will settle exactly where it should—into the waist. Measure the waist and cut a piece of one-inch-wide white grosgrain ribbon to that length plus several inches. Remove the elastic, replace it with the grosgrain, and then double-check that the grosgrain is comfortable. It should be snug but not too tight. The grosgrain will eventually be on the innermost layers of the bodice, so its fit now is very close to what the fit will be in the finished gown. (Eventually, the circumference of the outside of the gown will be approximately 3/4 inch larger than the inner circumference.)

When fitting the bodice, make sure that the waistline is accurately drawn on the muslin. Position the lower edge of the grosgrain on that drawn line. Note that the front half of the body is sometimes fleshier than the back half (there can be a discrepancy of up to an inch), and sometimes the back of the waist is a little lower than the front. There may be other idiosyncracies to take into account as well.

Next, pin the stay at the boning channels. The boning channels and the grosgrain are now anchored together, almost forming a little cage. (Technically speaking, the waistline stay should be on the inside of the muslin during the first muslin fitting, but getting at it to make adjustments is impossible. Also, pins on the inside of the muslin would dig into the wearer's waist. Therefore, for the sake of convenience, it is easier to place the waistline stay on the outside of the muslin. You will notice, then, a little puckering of the muslin between the points at which the waistline stay is pinned, as shown in Figure 3-9.)

THE MUSLIN'S ROLE IN FITTING

A solid understanding of fitting is a prerequisite for creating a couture gown. What follows are several aspects of fit that must be assessed when the gown is in the muslin stage.

The Fitting Session

At the first fitting, be sure to insist that the client wear the undergarments and shoes that she will use with the gown. A figure can change markedly depending on the undergarment, especially the position and fullness of the bust. Besides, you need to know not only how low the foundation garment lies in the front and back, but if there are straps and how wide they are. It's always worthwhile sending a client to a good foundation shop and asking her to come to the first fitting with a number of undergarments. Have her try them all, then select the one that is most flattering and that works best with the gown's design. As for the shoes, high heels will affect not only a skirt's length but a client's posture.

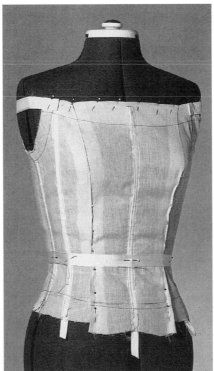

Figure 3-9: This muslin, after the initial fitting, contains adjustments along the upper edge, under the bust, along the lower edge. Notice the wide seam allowances and the waistline stay, which is pinned to the boning channels. When the muslin is taken apart, the alterations will be marked permanently.

Checklist for Evaluating Fit

☐ Vertical muslin centers are centered on the front and back of the body.

☐ Cross grains are parallel to the floor.

☐ Centers and side seams are perpendicular to the floor.

☐ Side seams are properly placed, coming directly down from the lowest point of the armhole.

☐ Waistline is accurately marked.

☐ Shoulder seams rest on top of the shoulders—unless the design purposely places them elsewhere.

☐ Princess seams run directly over the apex of the bust—unless the design purposely places them elsewhere.

☐ Darts come no closer than 1/2 to 1 inch from the apex of the bust.

☐ Base of the armhole is no more than 1/2 inch to 1 inch from the armpit.

☐ Fit is snug but not overly tight—up to two inches ease at the bust and up to one inch at the waist. A strapless or off-the-shoulder gown, however, should have less wearing ease than a garment with shoulders—usually no more than 3/4 inch at the bust and the waist.

☐ Long sleeves are the proper length—usually to the wrist bone, although sometimes a longer sleeve is preferred for an elongated line.

☐ Fitted sleeves are close to the arm, but there should be no undue strain on the fabric when the arm is bent; the fabric will pull uncomfortably at the elbow if the sleeve is too tight.

☐ Grainlines on sleeves are properly aligned. Looking at the bodice and sleeves from the side, the grainlines should be perpendicular to each other, the crosswise grain should be parallel to the floor, and the lengthwise grain should be perpendicular to the floor. Be careful that any adjustments to the sleeve and sleeve cap do not upset this crucial alignment (Figure 3-10).

☐ V on a long sleeve ends in a flattering position; if it is too far to the back of the hand, reposition it a little more toward the front of the hand (Figures 3-11 and 3-12).

☐ Elbow darts are properly placed, aligning with the bend in the elbow.

☐ Back (or side) opening closes without pulling or gaps; baste a zipper into the opening, or simply pin it closed; one advantage of a zipper (even if the gown will be later closed with buttons) is that it will evenly distribute the tautness along the back seam, eliminating gaps between pins.

☐ Boning is adequate and properly placed.

☐ The waistline stay is well fitted and rests just at the waistline.

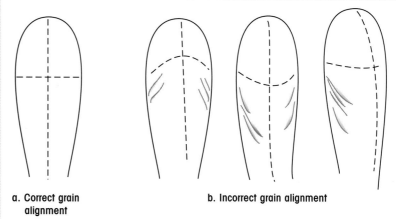

a. Correct grain alignment   **b. Incorrect grain alignment**

Figure 3-10: Less-than-perpendicular grainlines will cause wrinkles or drag lines to appear on the sleeves.

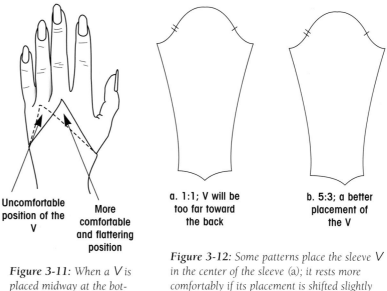

Uncomfortable position of the V   **More comfortable and flattering position**

Figure 3-11: When a V is placed midway at the bottom of the sleeve, it will feel as if it's pulling to the back of the hand.

a. 1:1; V will be too far toward the back   **b. 5:3; a better placement of the V**

Figure 3-12: Some patterns place the sleeve V in the center of the sleeve (a); it rests more comfortably if its placement is shifted slightly toward the front of the sleeve (b).

Many dressmakers like to fit the bodice by itself and then add the sleeves in a later fitting. Like so many things in fine sewing, it is a matter of preference, and as long as there is logic behind your decision, it is up to you.

Adjusting the Muslin

Many dressmakers expect to do at least two muslin fittings, so don't be dismayed if the fit isn't perfect the first time. It may only be in subsequent fittings that you begin to realize the subtleties of fit: How is the client's posture? How does she carry her arms? What is the slope of her shoulders? Is her neck short or long? What is the swell of her bust? Is hers a fleshy figure and, if so, just where is the flesh distributed? How much cleavage does she want to show?

Now that the wearer is actually wearing a version of her garment, she will have input, too. What seemed to her to be the perfect sleeve may now look much too large or much too small. She may find that what she thought was the perfect neckline is much too daring or not daring enough. She may find the skirt too full or not full enough. She may prefer pleats to gathers. So be prepared to change the muslin, sometimes drastically, because that's exactly why it's there.

When fitting a muslin, always keep twill tape or a narrow piece of ribbon or a piece of muslin or organza selvage to stabilize the neck edge. If left unstabilized, the neck will stretch and continue to stretch, especially in a fabric like muslin, because neck edges are often cut on the bias or at least have partial bias lines (Figures 3-13).

When adjusting the muslin, avoid the temptation to tighten a loose bodice by taking up all the slack in the center back seam. The extra fabric should be tightened up at more than one place, including the side seams. Taking it up only along the back seam will pull the side seams too far to the back, and the armhole will no longer be where it should be.

Use the basted seamlines as a guide when fitting. Even if you take a seam apart, the original seamlines are clearly marked, and having them as a point of

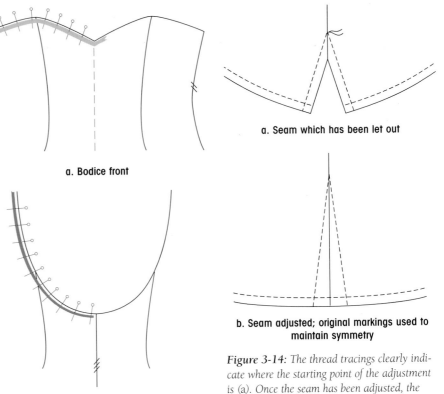

a. Bodice front

b. Bodice back

Figure 3-13: Not only does the twill tape keep the front edge from stretching, it pulls the fabric in, cupping it around the bust (a). The back neck edge is often on the bias; pin twill tape frequently to eliminate stretching (b).

departure will make adjusting a seam equally on both sides, for example, a clear and easy procedure. The same applies for shoulder seams, which are easy to over adjust to the point that the original starting point becomes unclear (Figure 3-14).

Working with the muslin is the perfect time to experiment with stiffenings for collars, drapes and other parts of the gown. With a portrait collar, for example, you can experiment with what might go inside: net (how many layers?), horsehair (how wide?), or a combination of the two. Perhaps batiste with some hidden boning would be a better choice.

On the muslin, permanently mark any adjustments in fit and design you've made to it. Mark the placement of the pins as you remove them and draw the adjustments. Make sure that your adjustments are accurate (if there is any question, baste the adjusted

a. Seam which has been let out

b. Seam adjusted; original markings used to maintain symmetry

Figure 3-14: The thread tracings clearly indicate where the starting point of the adjustment is (a). Once the seam has been adjusted, the original markings still serve as a guide, showing clearly an equal adjustment on both sides (b).

muslin together for a check). The adjusted shoulder seams should be right at the top of the shoulder, the redrawn line of a dropped waist should be exactly the same on both sides, and the increase or decrease made in a sleeve head should be graceful. As you finalize the adjustments, draw small slash marks through the old lines to keep from being confused by them (Figure 3-15).

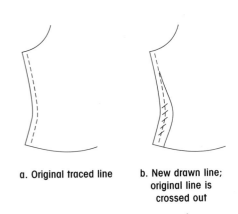

a. Original traced line

b. New drawn line; original line is crossed out

Figure 3-15: Mark adjustments on the muslin, crossing out the original lines to eliminate later confusion.

Once you are satisfied with the corrected muslin, (and remember, this may be only after a number of fittings, and major design changes), the muslin is ready to change roles—from that of your working garment to that of your pattern for cutting out and marking the fashion fabrics (Figure 3-16). So it must be dismantled and carefully pressed. Couture fashion fabrics are almost always laid out and cut one layer at a time, so having a full set of accurate pattern pieces is essential.

Bear in mind that there will be subsequent fittings of the garment, so you will have other opportunities for adjustments. Also, the gown will be of multiple layers—certainly the bodice will be—and certain treatments will affect fit. Heavy amounts of stitching to apply lace, for example, has the effect of "tightening up" the bodice. But that's

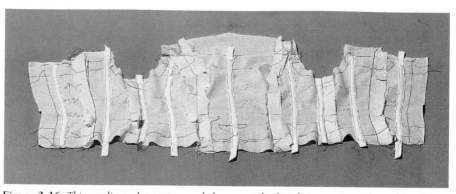

Figure 3-16: This muslin underwent several changes at the first fitting session. The neckline has been changed, the waist stay is accurately positioned, and the base of the bodice has been redrawn. There has been some shaping below the bust; the boning channels will be shortened later. The next step is to take apart the muslin and press it.

why this project is fitted, and fitted, and fitted again.

I hope you can now see the clear advantages of working with a muslin. Although much of the project lies ahead, the groundwork has been carefully and accurately laid, and the path is clearly marked.

The Bodice

The bodice is often the stylistic focus of the gown and, from a structural point of view, critical to its success. The bodice, therefore, presents the dressmaker with exciting and important decisions, both practical and aesthetic.

The most luxurious and well-planned outer fabrication cannot succeed without the proper inner structure. Nowhere is this more true than in the bodice. Strength must be built into the bodice, creating something that slims out the torso; supports the figure; enhances posture; flatters the wearer; supports sleeves, a collar, ornamentation, and a skirt of any style and weight without distortion; stays wrinkle-free; and allows a reasonable range of movement.

Structurally speaking, many articles of clothing hang from the shoulders. Jackets do, blouses do, sweaters do, many dresses do. Wedding gowns, however, with their tightly fitted torsos, are engineered differently. Obviously, an off-the-shoulder gown does not hang from the shoulders, but most other wedding gowns don't either. Their main support is located at the waist. The waist, circled by an inner waistband (waist stay) and accompanied by boning, is the logical anchor for a heavy gown. A heavy skirt, for example, hangs from the waist rather than from the shoulders or from the top of the bodice. While a tight bodice goes a long way in supporting a heavy gown, further inner support is often needed. For that reason, bodice structure must be solid, sturdy, and comfortable, and the support must be built into the inner layers of the bodice. Your tools for this job will be underlining, boning, and an inner waistband.

THE BODICE UNDERLINING

Underlining plays a critical role in the bodice's construction and design. While interfacing gives support to specific areas of a garment, such as the collar, jacket front, and cuffs, underlining's role is much broader. It provides a double, or even triple layer to the fashion fabric and is essential to the bodice's strength and integrity. The fashion fabric and the underlining are joined dur-

ing the early stages of garment construction, and thereafter, they are treated as a single layer of fabric.

Underlining provides a sturdy base for attaching lace, ornamentation, and heavy trims. It also camouflages the boning channels and other internal support elements and provides a base for internal stitches, which would otherwise show on the surface of the fashion fabric. It camouflages seam allowances and darts, which are especially noticeable with white fabrics and makes a firm base for sturdy closures. Underlining cuts down on creasing and wrinkling while providing a firm base for attaching the skirt as well as the collar, sleeves, and other fashion details.

In addition, underlinings allow you to use color to your advantage. You can whiten a fashion fabric with a white underlining, or you can make it less white with an off-white underlining. You can introduce colors; for example, you can intensify a pale pink fashion fabric by pairing it with a bright pink underlining, or you can make the color of the fashion fabric even more subtle by using a white underlining.

Every dressmaker has his or her favorite underlinings. I like to use heavy, tightly-woven cottons and often flannel in bodices, and I frequently use crinoline to support particularly heavy ornamentation. I may even use an extra layer in the center front if that area has a concentration of ornamentation. To select the best underlining for a particular gown, explore creative, unforeseen, even unorthodox combinations. If the underlining enhances the fabric, the design, the wearability, and the internal engineering, then it's a good, workable choice.

Analyze your underlinings the way you do your fashion fabric, and be sure to preshrink them, if necessary. There are many choices for underlinings and endless combinations. Some possibilities include:

- cotton batiste
- poly-cotton batiste of various thicknesses
- muslin
- cotton drill
- cotton twill
- pillow ticking
- duck
- silk organza
- single or double faced flannel
- crinoline (the original, heavily sized gauze)
- buckram

BODICE CONSTRUCTION

Here are the steps in constructing a bodice. Accuracy, patience, and careful machine and hand stitching will ensure your success.

Cut Out the Gown

To cut out the fashion fabric and the underlining(s), use the corrected, pressed muslin as your pattern. Take your full set of pattern pieces and lay them out in a single layer (Figure 3-17). You will need to repeat the layout and cutting process for the fashion fabric, for each layer of underlining, and eventually, for the lining.

Allow room for wide seam allowances—they will be trimmed later. You need wide allowances for possible adjustments in fit (remember, you will be working with multiple layers, and the addition of lace and surface embellishments may tighten up the bodice fabric). You will also need at least one-inch seam allowances along the top edges since they will function as facings, once they're turned back along the seamline.

If possible, place the center back pieces along a selvage, giving a nonraveling edge at the back of the bodice, which is usually the bodice opening. Allow an extension of at least two inches at the right center back for a placket if there will be buttons. You can add the placket later, but it is easy to allow fabric for one now.

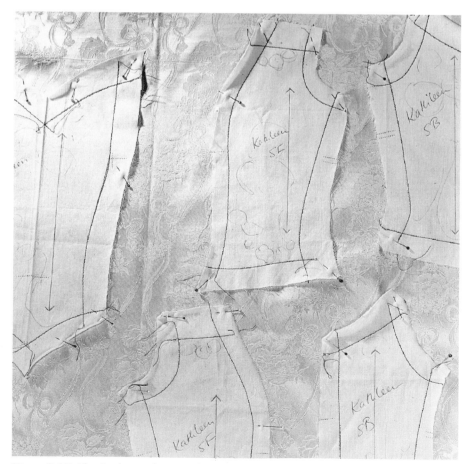

Figure 3-17: *The circular markings on the muslin indicate patterns in the damask, which must be taken into account. Notice the center crease in the fashion fabric, which wouldn't press out. It will need to be worked around.*

After cutting, don't mark the fashion fabric; the markings will be made on the underlining. In the case of multiple layers of underlinings, mark the underlining layer closest to the body. Mark as lightly as possible; check to make sure that the marks won't show through on the fashion fabric once the layers are joined. If necessary, use white tracing paper; it's difficult to see, but you'll be thread-tracing as soon as marking is finished. Be sure that notches or other markings appear only in the seam allowances. Don't mark the placement of the boning channels. It's too easy for the marks to show through, even with multiple layers, and you can easily and accurately place them visually. Grainlines needn't be marked on the underlining, as long as the grain has been accurately lined up with that of the muslin.

Apply the Boning Channels

After marking the underlining, you can add the boning channels. Be sure to preshrink them first, whether they are purchased cotton channels or grosgrain

---

Further Boning Considerations

Some bodices need boning below the waistline. The torso below the waist is often fleshier than the torso above the waist, and undergarments that stop at the waist may create a visible change in silhouette right at the waistline. While adequate underlining and proper fit will help the bodice lie flat and even below the waist, boning is often the only way to ensure a smooth line throughout the torso. Here are some bodice styles that can benefit from boning below the waistline.

Basque Waist from the Natural Waist. Basque waists are unstable because there is nothing to hold them down, especially if the skirt goes out (as in a fluffy tulle skirt) as opposed to down (as in a heavy satin skirt). Strengthen the point of a basque waist with strong underlining in addition to boning which points down into the V; one bone may be sufficient, but three are more likely the answer. Sometimes even five are required (Figure 3-18a).

Basque Waist from a Dropped Waist. Usually, the V in this style bodice doesn't drop more than four or five inches below the natural waist. Strengthen and stabilize the V with boning that goes all the way down to the base of the bodice. Boning will smooth out the whole silhouette and encourage the V to stay in place (Figure 3-18b).

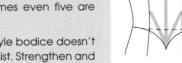
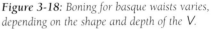

Figure 3-18: Boning for basque waists varies, depending on the shape and depth of the V.

Graduated Waist, Dropped Waist, Softened V Waist. These are similar in that they all extend below the waist. Although the weight of the skirt will encourage them to stay in place, they need boning below the waist to ensure that they don't ride up (Figure 3-19).

Some garments benefit from a separate inner foundation.

Inner Corselette. Sometimes, an inner foundation, markedly tighter than the fashion fabric, is necessary. Picture a strapless trapeze dress: It needs something to hold it up. Apart from where it is joined along the top edge, it floats away from the body. A foundation, made of very firm underlining, is constructed to the waistline, complete with boning and a waist stay. Then the fashion fabric garment and the inner foundation are joined along the top edge, their only common edge (Figure 3-20). If the discrepancy between the fashion fabric and the foundation is minimal, they can share the same closure; usually, though, the foundation closes independently of the fashion fabric. The foundation closes first, with its own zipper or with a row of lingerie hooks. The fashion fabric then closes over it. The construction of this kind of an inner corselette is detailed in the Glamorous Blue Gown in Part IV.

a. Graduated Waist   b. Dropped Waist   c. Softened V Waist

Figure 3-19: Boning stabilizes the bodice in each of these three styles of dropped waists.

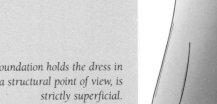
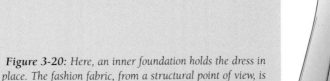

Figure 3-20: Here, an inner foundation holds the dress in place. The fashion fabric, from a structural point of view, is strictly superficial.

ribbon, or whether you've made them yourself.

Place the channel and boning as close to the upper seamline of the bodice as possible, but not so close that it makes a bump along the top edge once the seam allowance is folded over. Check for this along the bottom edge of the boning casing as well; the boning mustn't protrude into the seam allowance. Then, stitch the channels to the underlining nearest the body, starting at the lower edge on one side, going up and over the top, and finishing at the lower edge on the other side (Figure 3-21). As the bones themselves are removed while working on the bodice, you'll close the channels at their base after putting the boning in for the final time. Be sure that the boning is reasonably snug, but not too tight, inside the boning channels.

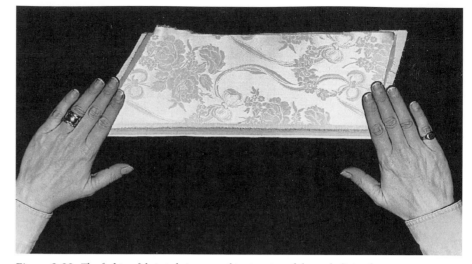

Figure 3-22: The fashion fabric is being spread taut on top of the underlining layers.

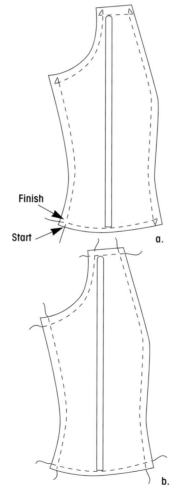

Figure 3-21: Leave bottom edge open when attaching the boning channels; it will be closed later when the boning is inserted for the final time.

Hand Baste the Underlining

The next step is to hand baste the underlining to the fashion fabric. Not only will basting stitches hold all the layers together, but they will mark the fashion fabric, providing clearly marked bodice sections. Join the layers, checking for stray threads and bits of fluff between the layers before basting them together. Smooth out the layers, with the fashion fabric on top. The fashion fabric must be taut. The undermost underlining layer may appear slightly less than taut (Figure 3-22).

Start basting at one bottom corner of the piece and follow the contours around and down the other side, finishing with the lower edge. Check the tautness of the fashion fabric as you go,

and restitch as necessary; check a final time before basting across the bottom edge (Figure 3-23). Some dressmakers baste outside the stitching line; I baste on it, for the sake of accuracy and to completely eliminate any slippage (Figure 3-24). Machine basting is tempting but the fabric layers will inevitably shift.

Figure 3-23: Baste the layers together with one continuous thread, stitching to the end of the seamline before turning the corner; there mustn't be any pulling when going around corners (a). Or stitch each edge with a separate thread, running it all the way to the end of the seamline (b).

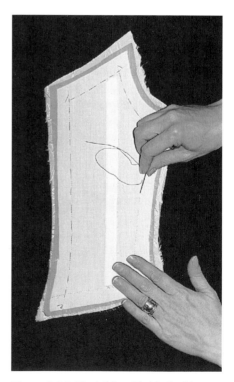

Figure 3-24: The left hand holds the fabrics flat and keeps them from shifting while the right hand bastes. Although dark thread is used here for the sake of contrast, matching thread should be used.

Many wedding gown bodices have princess seams, which eliminates worrying about darts. For bodices that do have darts, be sure to line up the layers through the point of the dart. Then, as you did on the muslin, baste three rows of stitches at each dart: one down the center (this line is critical) and one down each leg of the dart (Figure 3-25). Such basting ensures that the layers, even if they are slippery, will work as one. As with the other carbon markings on the underlining, be sure there is no show-through, especially in this particularly exposed location.

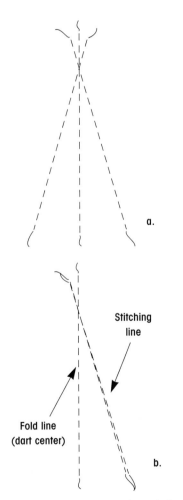

Figure 3-25: Trace the dart on the underlining with white tracing paper, then baste all layers together. Extend the lines beyond the point of the dart, for stability. Use silk thread if marking on satin or crepe. The dart is ready to stitch (a). When stitching, the basting stitches on the fold line are visible, as are the basting stitches on the right dart leg (b). Remove all basting stitches carefully after stitching the dart.

Baste the Garment Sections

Now you're ready to baste the garment sections together (Figure 3-26). If there are princess seams over the bust, you may want to slip baste them, especially if you are working with a slippery or bulky fabric. At this point, the bodice must be fitted (the client must wear the proper undergarments). Remember that adding lace or ornamentation may subtly tighten the garment, so allow for that. Any minor adjustments can often be taken care of later at the back seam. At the fitting, be sure to check the following: the position of the seamline at the top of the bodice front and back, the depth of the front V, the shape around and under the bust, the ease around the armhole, and the marking of the lower edge of the bodice (not only for a basque waist, but for the placement of the entire skirt).

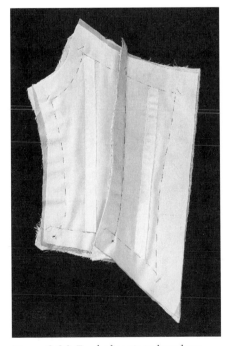

Figure 3-26: Two bodice pieces have been basted together in preparation for a fitting.

As the boning and underlining(s) will be in place at this point, baste the waistline stay into place, following the placement on the muslin and aligning the base of the grosgrain ribbon along the waistline. During the fitting, pin twill tape to the top of the bodice to indicate the amount of ease and its eventual placement The twill tape that was used during the muslin fitting can be used here, or new twill tape can be placed. Before stitching the garment together, remove and set aside the twill tape, carefully noting its exact placement for later attachment.

Stitch the Garment Sections

Once you're satisfied with the fit, stitch the garment sections together. Don't backtrack at the beginnings and ends of the seamlines; this can cause puckering. Instead, secure the seamlines by making sure each one extends beyond the cross points. After stitching the seams, remove the basting. Then, trim the seam allowances to about 1/2 inch and carefully remove the seam allowances of bulky or stiff underlinings—flannel and crinoline, especially.

Next, press the bodice, using a pressing cloth—a piece of silk organza is ideal: It is transparent and can take high heat. Press patiently and firmly—you'll be amazed at how careful pressing can improve the appearance of the garment.

Sandwich press first by pressing down on both sides of each unopened seam to meld the stitches. Then spread the seams open with your fingernail to avoid pressing in tiny creases along the seamlines. Carefully press open the seams, clipping as necessary and using a pressing ham on any shaped seams. If your seam allowances seem bulky, consider staggering the places where you clip the fashion fabric and the underlining (Figure 3-27). Staggering will

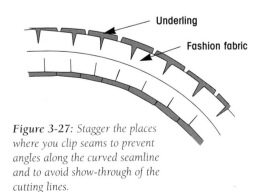

Figure 3-27: Stagger the places where you clip seams to prevent angles along the curved seamline and to avoid show-through of the cutting lines.

also eliminate show-through on the fashion fabric.

After trimming and pressing the seams, catch stitch them to keep them open and flat. It is essential to catch stitch at least the princess seams in the front over the bust curve. In addition, it's a good idea to catch stitch fabrics that ravel and seams that cannot seem to stay flat. The catch stitches go from the seam allowance onto the underlining—not through to the fashion fabric.

Finish the Top Edges

Staystitch along the seamlines at the top edges, being careful that seam allowances remain open and flat. Reinforce the center V by shortening the staystitches on either side of the center point. Clip vertically into the V, and clip elsewhere along the top seam if necessary (Figure 3-28). If you must clip along the top seam allowance, do so carefully so that there are no visible distortions from the clipping once the seam allowance is folded inward.

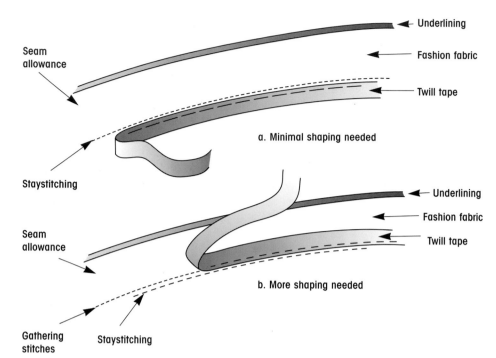

Figure 3-29: Twill tape should be attached to the top seamline of the bodice. If shaping needs are minimal (a), attach the tape to the underlining with a running stitch through all layers except the outermost. When more shaping is needed (b), add a line of gathering stitches just above the seamline and rest the twill tape on the stitching line, holding it in place with a running stitch on the gathering line.

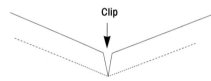

Figure 3-28: The top edge has been staystitched and reinforced at the V. Notice the shortened stitches on either side of the center. All layers will be clipped right down to the staystitching line.

For stability and shaping, apply twill tape along the top seamline of the bodice. Unless the top edge is straight across, it will be at least somewhat off grain and, therefore, unstable. Twill tape will not only prevent stretching, it will help cup the top edge of the bodice around the bust. Further, it will encourage the boning to stay close to the chest along the top edge of the bodice.

The amount of ease that must be worked in depends on the fashion fabric, the degree of bias at the top edge of the bodice, the position of that edge, and the fullness of the bust. On a V-front bodice with off-the-shoulder sleeves, for example, the amount of ease

will be between 3/8 and 5/8 inch from the center front to each side. If shaping is minimal, simply pin in the ease as you apply the twill tape. Then, secure the tape onto the underlining just at or below the seamline, with a small running stitch. The twill tape's top edge should rest just on the stitching line (Figure 3-29a). If more shaping is needed, machine stitch a row of gathering stitches just above the seamline, gather as needed, and, using a running stitch, sew the twill tape on by hand just at or above the seamline (Figure 3-29b).

If the top edge of the bodice back is off grain, stabilize it as well. Remember, though, that when the wearer's arms move forward, the back must expand. The wearer will feel as if she's encased in a straightjacket if a straight back edge is stabilized too much. You must stabilize a deep and plunging V at the back, but otherwise use twill tape very carefully there.

Along the seamline at the top of the bodice, turn down the edges, with the staystitching just inside the folded edge. Press the edges carefully, and catch stitch them firmly in place (Figure 3-30).

Figure 3-30: Twill tape is visible on the top left of the bodice, while the seam allowance of the top right of the bodice has been turned down and is held in place with catch stitching. The boning channels are in place, and one princess seam has been pressed, notched, and catch stitched. (Dark stitches are used here for the sake of identification.)

Attach the Waistline Stay

Secure the waistline stay to the boning channels, leaving it free at the center back waist (or side, if that is where the bodice opening is) where it will fasten independently of the gown's closure (Figure 3-31). Attach a pair of hooks and eyes or a single bar hook for the closing. Also, pad the closing so that the hooks don't dig into the wearer's back (Figure 3-32). It should be snug, but comfortable, and it should not create a ridge that is visible from the outside of the garment.

THE BODICE LINING

Line the bodice before attaching the sleeves and skirt (the boning can be slipped out of its channels and inserted later). A well-fitted, beautifully constructed lining is one of the most important finishing details of a fine gown. Not only will the lining camouflage the often intensive inner structure of a well-engineered bodice, but it will impart a feeling of luxury, showing that the inside of the garment can look as beautiful as the outside. From a practical point of view, the lining's smooth surface will make the gown easier to put on and to wear; and the extra layer of silk will help absorb perspiration and minimize abrasion on the inside of the bodice.

Construct the Lining

Remember that the lining is a mirror image rather than an exact copy of the fashion fabric; its wrong side will face the wrong side of the garment. As you construct the lining, accurately incorporate any changes that have been made during fitting. Bodies are rarely symmetrical, so be sure that changes to the muslin are made on the proper side (right or left) of the lining.

Cut the lining from the corrected muslin pattern. Mark the lining so that the tracings don't show through. When working with white lining fabric, white tracing paper must be used. Good lining choices include spun silk, china silk, silk crepe de chine, and silk charmeuse.

Assemble and stitch the lining. Then trim, clip and press all seams. Leave a wide seam allowance at the right center back seamline. Staystitch the neckline along the seamline. Trim and clip the seam allowance, then press it toward the inside of the lining so that the staystitching is barely out of sight from the right side. Make two vertical buttonholes close to the center back line if there is to be a waistline stay; this is where the waist stay will emerge so that it can hook. Reinforce the buttonholes with small pieces of silk organza.

Insert the Lining

Fell stitch the lining in place along the neckline. Baste it in place around the armscyes. This row of basting will serve as a stitching guide when you're inserting the sleeves.

To finish the left center back, fold the lining along the center back line (the same line the loops have been sewn on)

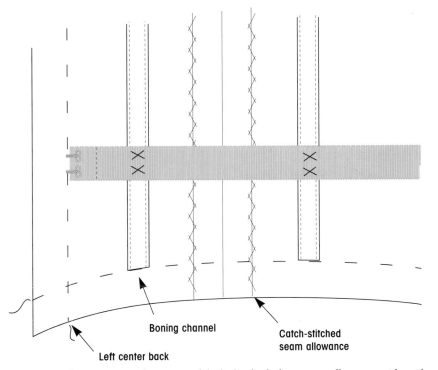

Boning channel

Catch-stitched seam allowance

Left center back

Figure 3-31: *This inner view of a portion of the bodice back shows seam allowances with catch stitching and a waistline stay that has been tacked to the boning channels.*

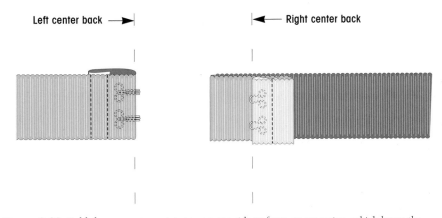

Left center back ➡️   ⬅️ **Right center back**

Figure 3-32: *Fold the grosgrain waist stay on one side to form an extension, which keeps the hooks from digging into the wearer's back. When closed, the centers will abut.*

Figure 3-33: The lining has been assembled and fell stitched in place around the neckline and down the center back. It is basted at the armscye along the stitching line. The waist stay, which will be finished with hooks and eyes later, emerges from an opening in the lining.

and fell stitch in place. Leave the bottom few inches unstitched and finish them once the skirt is in place (Figure 3-33).

Finish the right back bodice with an extension, or a placket, using the seam allowance. If there is not enough seam allowance, you can add an extension. Wrap the lining around the fashion fabric, fold under its raw edge, and fell stitch it in place. As with the left back bodice, leave the bottom few inches unstitched and finish them once the skirt is in place.

Tack the remaining lining seam, the lower edge along the base of the bodice, in place once the skirt has been sewn on. Place a row of prick stitches along the top edge of the bodice. No matter how well-fitted, a lining can ride up, and this simple step will guarantee that it doesn't. A carefully placed row of prick stitches, about ½ inch below the top edge of the bodice, catching all layers of fabric except the outermost, will anchor the lining to the bodice.

COMMON BODICE STYLES

The style of a bodice determines its engineering and construction requirements. Here are a number of common bodice styles, along with important information to consider when constructing them. The bodices are categorized here as covering the shoulder, off the shoulder, and sleeveless.

Bodices that Cover the Shoulders

V-FRONT AND -BACK. One of the trickiest silhouettes to stabilize is that with a V-front, a deep V-back, and heavy sleeves. There are a few things you can do, however, to help keep things in place. Stabilize the front and back neck edges with twill tape, and use a wide piece of interfacing, cut along the straight grain, along the front and back V seamlines (in addition to the underlining), to stabilize them further (Figure

3-34). Also, shape the shoulder seam somewhat to make it "settle in" better on the shoulder bone (Figure 3-35).

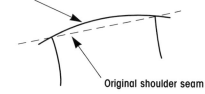

Figure 3-35: Shoulder seams can be subtly shaped to curve around the shoulder bones, encouraging them to "settle in" around the shoulder.

V-BACK. A deep back V is not a particular challenge as long as the front is reasonably high; if it isn't, extreme measures are required. The problem is keeping the shoulders in place. In addition to underlining and twill tape, consider adding further inner support in the form of elastic, which is anchored to the waist stay. What you are creating is similar to suspenders, but on the inside. Use inner elastic carefully, though, because its presence can cause the waist to ride up unevenly, distorting

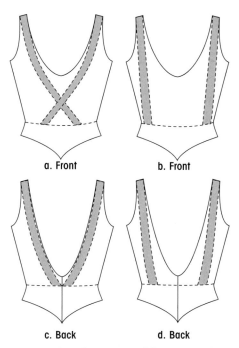

a. Front   b. Front

c. Back   d. Back

Figure 3-36: These suggested front and back elastic placements will encourage low front and back Vs to stay in place. They are anchored at the waist.

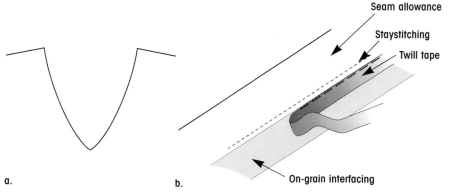

a.   b.

Figure 3-34: The V bodice is slightly bowed. It is more flattering than a true V (a). Add interfacing along the top seamline of the bodice, in addition to twill tape, to keep the V in place (b).

other parts of the gown. Elastic can be placed in a number of ways. With experimentation, careful placement, and just the right amount of tension, elastic can prove very useful (Figure 3-36). Tack it as necessary.

SCOOP. Stabilize a scoop neckline. Whether it will be self-faced or faced with the lining, a separate facing, or even a strip of bias, the scoop must be absolutely smooth. Be sure to stagger the notches. Frequent, shallow notches are better than fewer, deeper notches. Catch stitch the seam allowance firmly to the underlining (Figure 3-37). If a facing is being used, understitch it.

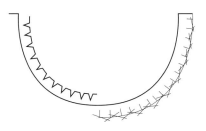

Figure 3-37: On the left side, this scoop neckline has frequent, shallow notches (areas that have been clipped). On the right side, catch stitching holds the turned down seam allowance, which serves as the facing, in place.

SWEETHEART. This is a beautiful neckline when it is clearly shaped and stays in place, but it loses its beauty if it sags or is distorted in any way. So, the same considerations taken into account for the V and scoop necklines apply here. Also be sure that the underlining at the shaped part of the neckline is sufficiently firm to maintain the sweetheart shape (Figure 3-38).

Figure 3-38: Add interfacing at the neck edge to keep the sweetheart shape stable.

JEWEL. The jewel neckline must be, most of all, comfortable. With a heavy gown pulling at it, the neckline can be torturously tight, tugging at the throat for hours. Your muslin fittings will have guided you in the placement of the neckline, but be sure that it is comfortable, that the shoulder seams are right at the top of the shoulders, and that the bodice hangs evenly from the shoulders, not from the neck. Whichever finish you use on the neck, be sure that it doesn't tighten up the neckline or distort it—some bias finishes actually rise above the neckline and make it tighter than expected (Figure 3-39).

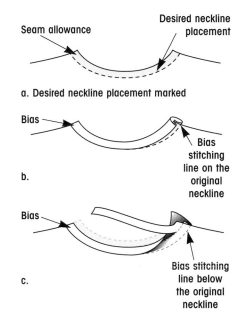

Seam allowance

Desired neckline placement

a. Desired neckline placement marked

Bias

b.

Bias stitching line on the original neckline

Bias

c.

Bias stitching line below the original neckline

Figure 3-39: The jewel neckline can be tight if it is not finished properly. Sewing the bias on the original neckline (b) results in a higher, tighter neckline (the bias rises above the original neckline) because the folded bias binding covers the seam allowance. Sewing the bias below the neckline (c) results in a neckline equal to that of the original desired neckline. Trim the seam allowance before folding over the bias and stitching it in place.

BOAT, OR BATEAU. This is a wonderfully clean, elegant neckline. It seldom goes perfectly straight across, so be sure that the shaping is flattering and that the shoulders are exactly where they should be. Otherwise, the bodice will pull or sag across the front. Be sure the neckline is adequately underlined so that it doesn't sag (Figure 3-40).

Figure 3-40: Use a strip of interfacing at the neck edge to eliminate sagging.

SQUARE. Shoulder placement is critical for this neckline, which needs inner support to maintain its square shape. Be sure to reinforce the corners—there mustn't be the slightest hint of puckering. You may want to interface the square to ensure that it stays firm, especially at the horizontal seam across the upper bust (Figure 3-41).

Figure 3-41: Reinforce and clip the corners; consider adding interfacing (a strip of horsehair), or even boning (placed horizontally along the neck edge) to encourage stability.

WEDDING BAND COLLAR. For this neckline, the shoulder seams must be accurately placed, and they must follow any curves and slopes in the shoulders. The wedding band collar must rest gently around the neck and not pull in any way. Line the collar with a soft fabric (a scrap of bias-cut silk charmeuse is ideal) to give an extra bit of comfort (Figure 3-42).

Figure 3-42: Consider lining the collar with a bias strip of silk charmeuse or something similarly soft.

Off-the-Shoulder Bodices

V-NECK. Boning, underlining, and careful shaping with twill tape are essential for maintaining a pleasing V shape. Although the elastic in the sleeves will help support the bodice, the sleeves will also pull on it, so the bodice's internal support must be firm. Consider adding small pieces of boning to counteract any pulling at the neckline; horizontal stretch lines at the top of the bodice will spoil the beauty of the entire bodice (Figure 3-43).

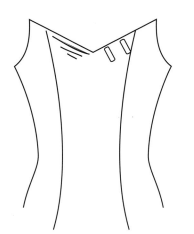

Figure 3-43: Add small pieces of boning to the bodice edge if there is any horizontal pulling.

STRAIGHT ACROSS. Boning and underlining are the key to maintaining shape, but shaping with twill tape isn't necessary as the neckline goes straight across. You may want to include some interfacing (horsehair works well) along the neckline to ensure a clean upper bodice line (Figure 3-44).

Figure 3-44: Consider a strip of interfacing or horsehair to guarantee a clean edge.

SLIGHTLY CURVED. Apart from the necessary boning and underlining, the curve in this neckline may need a little

extra stability. Easing probably isn't necessary, but consider a little interfacing across the top edge if there is the slightest hint of pulling, distortion, or sagging (Figure 3-45). As with any scoop neck, notch carefully to ensure an absolutely smooth line.

Figure 3-45: To keep this neckline smooth looking, make the notches even, frequent, and shallow; consider interfacing for support.

STRAPLESS. Adequate boning, firm underlining, a secure waistline stay, and shaping at the top bodice edge will guarantee a comfortable, flattering strapless bodice. Eliminating any of these elements will compromise the success of the bodice. Extend the twill tape shaping all the way to the side seams, tightening it as much as ³/4 inch per side (Figure 3-46).

SHAWL COLLAR AND PORTRAIT COLLAR. These are variations on a V-neck bodice and are basically superficial design elements which must be placed over a firm supporting garment (Figure 3-47). The collars themselves need internal support and a firm bodice underneath. As shawl and portrait collars are meant to curve gracefully around the shoulders, they should be cut on the bias; otherwise, they won't curve well, especially along the top folded edge. Consider adding internal support and shaping with wide horsehair, which guarantees a beautiful, uncrushable curve. Catch stitch the horsehair in place (Figure 3-48). Net (stiff can-can netting) is another good collar stiffening; use as many layers as necessary, and catch stitch them in place. If using multiple layers of net, cut each layer separately rather than

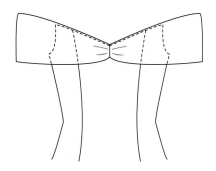

Figure 3-47: A portrait collar must rest on a firm bodice foundation; be sure the collar itself is well supported with underlining(s).

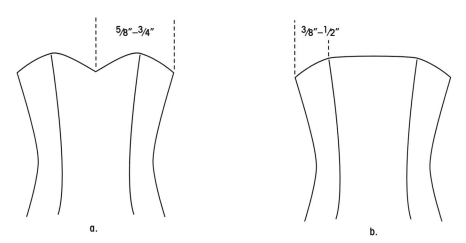

Figure 3-46: Making sure the top of the princess seam is attractively and symmetrically shaped, ease the top of the bodice as needed. Here are some guidelines for incorporating ease into the top edge so that it cups the breast. The shaping may be subtle or dramatic.

a.   b.

5/8"–3/4"   3/8"–1/2"

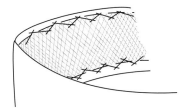

Figure 3-48: Use wide horsehair, held with a loose catch stitch, inside the collar to guarantee a beautiful, uncrushable curve.

Sleeveless Bodices

Be sure to staystitch around the armscye to stabilize the seam. The armhole can be finished with bias binding, with a shaped facing (use the muslin for an accurate pattern), or with a strip of bias that folds to the inside and is fell stitched to the underlining (Figure 3-49). The armhole can also be finished in the manner of the top bodice edges: staystitched, clipped, pressed in, catch stitched, and covered with the lining (the lining is then prick stitched to keep it in place).

doubling it by folding it along the top edge. A folded net edge won't shape into a smooth curve.

Figure 3-49: Turn the inside edge of the bias strip under, and fell stitch it to the underlining of a sleeveless bodice.

The Sleeves

Although the sleeves must be technically sound, the stylistic possibilities they offer are endless. From the designer's point of view, the sleeve is a perfect opportunity to combine form (often wonderfully inventive and elaborate form) with function.

Sleeves are not limited to the close-fitting silhouette required of most bodices, nor do they have an overly complicated inner structure. The fabric requirements aren't enormous, so weight isn't usually a concern; nor is the primary purpose of the sleeve to keep the bride's arms warm or covered.

Well-thought-out sleeves can enhance the proportions of the gown, widen the bride's shoulders, and balance a full skirt. They can showcase any of a number of embellishments and ornamentation, further develop a gown's theme, and use beautiful and creative fabric combinations. Sleeves are fun to design, manageable to create, and they add enormously to the overall appeal of the gown.

Sleeves often combine fabrics, and it is those combinations, sometimes unexpected, which add charm to their silhouette. Picture a gigot (leg-of-mutton) sleeve with beautifully textured silk douppioni sprinkled with clusters of pearls at the top and Alençon lace on the fitted lower part, or lace at the top and the douppioni on the lower part. Think of a long, slim silk organza sleeve with a narrow bias-cut satin cuff, or a simple piece of elastic at the top of the arm clustered with softly shaded silk roses. The combinations are endless.

SET-IN SLEEVES

For all their variations, there is terminology that sleeves have in common, and there are technical components that they share as well. The *underarm line,* or the bicep line (the widest horizontal point of the sleeve), divides the sleeve into the *sleeve cap* (the area above the bicep line) and the *sleeve body* (the area below the bicep line). A well-fitted,

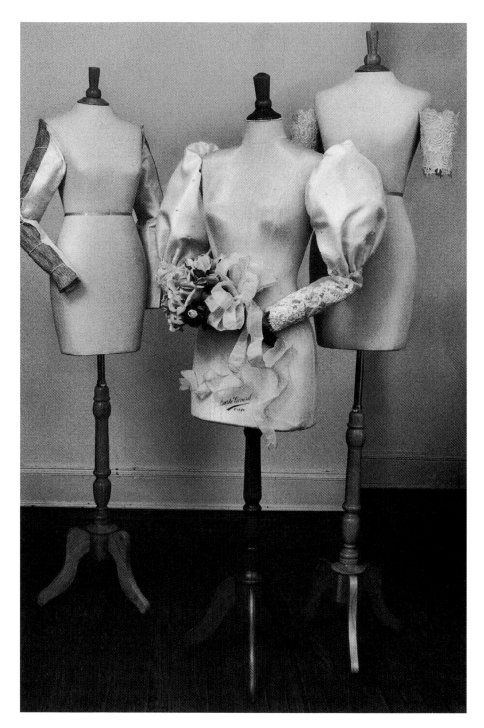

slim sleeve has one, two, or three darts at the elbow; otherwise, ease is built into the back sleeve seam at the elbow point (Figure 3-50). The sleeve cap is where fullness, or loft, is accommodated. Be sure that any alteration to the sleeve cap, to add or diminish loft, slopes gracefully from the top of the cap down into the armscye on both sides (Figure 3-51).

Considerations for Sleeves

Here are some general considerations to taken into account when planning the sleeves:

- What underlining, if any, should be used? As the sleeves aren't supporting anything, you don't need the extraordinary measures which sometimes need to be taken with bodices. Also, there is no boning to conceal.

- What seam finishes are best? Many sleeves are sheer, so seam finishes and sleeve heads may be visible. A beautifully constructed sheer sleeve head in a sheer sleeve is perfectly acceptable. However, seam allowances must be finished carefully, as sleeves are often either sheer or unlined.

- How tight can the sleeve be? Sheer fabrics can be weak and there is strain on them at the elbow and hinge points of the armscye if the sleeve is tightly fitted. Strike the right balance between beautifully slim and dangerously tight.

- How might a grainline change affect the sleeve? A highly textured silk douppioni, for example, is beautiful when placed on the bias and allows the wearer wonderful ease of movement, especially at the elbow. The hem of a short sleeve, gently folded under, will curve beautifully if the sleeve is cut on the bias.

- What special attention might be given to the lower sleeve? The wrist is a focal point, of course—the hands, the ring and the bouquet all attract attention—and deserves special consideration on a long sleeve: careful placement of lace motifs, a beautiful edging or trim, a gracefully proportioned bow.

- Should the sleeves be lined? If so, add the lining before the sleeves are sewn to the bodice.

example). While the underlining may give adequate support, the choices for extra help range from an added layer or two of silk organza to multiple layers of net, and even wide horsehair.

Sleeve heads are either part of the internal structure of the sleeve or a separate component. Internal sleeve heads are formed by supporting the sleeve cap internally beyond whatever help the underlining gives. A layer of net, for example, can cover the sleeve cap, extending as far down as necessary. For further support at the top, add a second layer that doesn't go down as far as the first (Figure 3-52). These multiple layers are usually easy to gather—net is mostly air, as is lace, so these layers are not bulky or difficult to deal with (Figure 3-53).

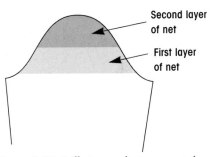

Figure 3-52: Stiffening can be incorporated into the sleeve cap area. The net layer(s) will scarcely be visible, even through transparent fabrics.

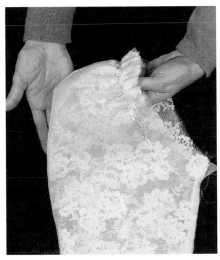

Figure 3-53: A lace and silk organza sleeve is seen from the inside. There are two layers of net in the sleeve cap area (one extends lower than the other). Here, the organza not only adds strength, but also acts as a buffer between the net and the shoulder. The layers in order from the outside are: Alençon lace, net, net, silk organza.

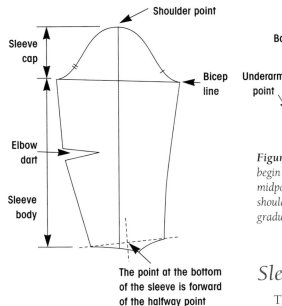

Figure 3-50: This is a standard, fitted long sleeve with an elbow dart and a V at the wrist. Notice that the point at the bottom of the sleeve is slightly forward from the halfway point.

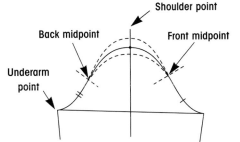

Figure 3-51: Sleeve cap alterations usually begin at the front and back midpoints (the midpoint is halfway between the top of the shoulder and the underarm). Make alterations gradually and gracefully.

Sleeve Heads

There are as many variations of sleeve heads as there are sleeves. The purpose of a sleeve head is to fill the gap between the wearer's shoulder and the outer sleeve silhouette. The demands vary according to fabrication (both fashion fabric and underlining), sleeve length (a shorter sleeve is lighter and, therefore, easier to support), and the desired effect (soft gathers gently held in place, or crisp pleats firmly held in place, for

To create an internal net sleeve head, use three rows of gathering stitches (one on the seamline, and the other two in the seam allowance). Once gathered, press the seam allowance flat to reduce bulk and encourage the gathers to stay in place (Figure 3-54). If there is a lining (many sleeves are not lined), gather it at the same time the sleeve cap is gathered. Not only is this an efficient way to join the sleeve to its lining, the lining creates a buffer between the wearer and the sometimes scratchy stiffening fabric (Figure 3-55).

Figure 3-54: Once an arm is inside the sleeve, a determination can be made whether the internal support is adequate. It should be in this case, but an additional separate sleeve head can always be made and added.

Figure 3-55: The net inside this guipure sleeve gives enough support. The four layers—guipure, silk shantung, net, spun silk lining—have been treated as one.

The chief advantage of separate sleeve heads is that they are infinitely variable, even after the sleeve has been designed. Loft can be added or taken away, and the subtleties of proportion after the sleeve is in place can be addressed (Figure 3-56). You can make more than one sleeve head for a sleeve: For example, a soft and puffy silk organza one might go on top to fill out the uppermost part of a sleeve cap, working in tandem with something firmer underneath. A half-moon of soft satin placed between the sleeve head(s) and the wearer will act as a buffer, ensuring no roughness next to the wearer's skin.

Figure 3-56: Here, a football-shaped piece of net is folded in half and gathered. The semicircular edge will rest on the seam line. The stiff edges of the net's seam allowance are contained within a satin binding. There is also a satin half-moon to keep the net from irritating the wearer.

Types of Set-In Sleeves

TULIP SLEEVE. The tulip sleeve is an easy-to-create variation of the short sleeve; the split allows good range of arm movement, and the sleeve resumes its shape once the arm is lowered. Mark all the components (fashion fabric, lining, underlining) carefully; the number of sleeve pieces is double that of a one-

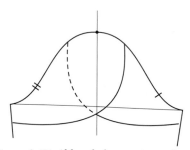

Figure 3-57: Although the two pieces of a tulip sleeve must cross evenly at the center of the sleeve, the amount of overlap and the shape of the curve are matters of taste.

piece sleeve (Figure 3-57). When constructing the sleeve, overlap it in either direction—front over back, or back over front. Extend any edging, such as a border lace or an ornamented trim, up to the topmost part of the sleeve, even on the underneath part. If the fashion fabric is heavy, this sleeve can be bulky once the overlap is in place. Remember this when considering underlining and sleeve cap support. To lessen bulk, you may want to reduce the sleeve cap, creating fewer gathers, and you may want to consider pleats as an alternative. On one hand, the thickness of the sleeve may help it support itself; on the other hand, the entire sleeve will be heavier.

BELL SLEEVE. The bell sleeve flares out from the center of the top of the sleeve, much in the manner of a circular skirt. On the flat pattern, the hem will curve; once worn, it will hang evenly (Figure 3-58).

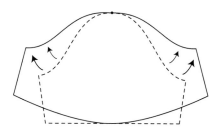

Figure 3-58: The bell sleeve flares out from the standard sleeve. Although the armhole edge is shifted, the armhole measurement remains the same, and the hem curves to accommodate the added circumference at the bottom of the sleeve. Note that the angle of the armhole and the underarm seam remain constant. The added fullness is distributed around the entire sleeve.

TRUMPET SLEEVE. The trumpet sleeve usually starts out tight and then flares at, above, or below the elbow. The flare can be an extension of the upper part of the sleeve or it can come from a separate piece of fabric. The flare can be of a consistent length, or it can vary to accommodate design and wearability. It can, for example, be shorter toward the front edge of the forearm, and be longer toward the outer edge of the forearm (Figure 3-59).

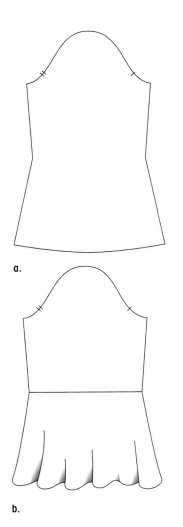

a.

b.

Figure 3-59: The trumpet sleeve also flares, but its distinctive shape starts below a fitted upper sleeve. In its simplest form, the one-piece sleeve flares out (a); in more complicated versions, the flare is so dramatic that it is formed by a separate piece, and often multiple layers, of fabric and/or lace (b).

CAP SLEEVE. All of this sleeve is contained in the cap area of the sleeve; hence its name (Figure 3-60). The cap sleeve can have a small underarm seam,

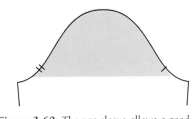

Figure 3-60: The cap sleeve allows a good range of motion; the sleeve is not attached around the entire armscye.

or it can be so abbreviated that it doesn't. This abbreviated form allows good movement, as the sleeve isn't anchored around the entire armscye.

GIGOT, OR LEG-OF-MUTTON, SLEEVE. The gigot sleeve consists of a full, gathered upper sleeve joined to a tight, fitted lower sleeve. It allows for wonderful fabric combinations as well as a good range of movement—the fullness of the top part doesn't compromise the tight fit of the lower part. Create a casing for elastic where the two parts of the sleeve join, to keep the lower part of the sleeve from slipping down the arm and to keep the top part of the sleeve nicely rounded. Use an internal stay (a piece of twill tape or narrow ribbon) from the top of

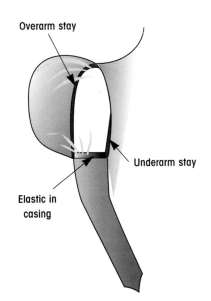

Figure 3-61: The gigot, or leg-of-mutton, sleeve maintains its shape not only through careful fit and construction, but with the assistance of elastic and inner stays. The elastic gently grips the upper arm, and the stays keep the sleeve in place without any sort of strain, allowing it to remain full and beautifully shaped.

the shoulder down the outside edge of the arm, secured to the base of the upper part of the sleeve, for the same reasons. Similarly, place another stay from the center of the underarm directly down to the base of the upper part of the sleeve (Figure 3-61).

PUFF SLEEVE. A puff sleeve can be off or on the shoulder and is usually held in place with elastic at both the top and bottom edges. The casing can be visible or it can be turned under. Fullness and loft can be added with variations in both width and height; experimentation with these proportions, as well as with underlining, will reveal the best combinations (Figure 3-62).

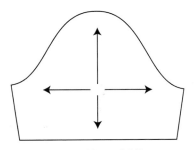

Figure 3-62: For additional fullness, increase both the width and depth of a puff sleeve. Use elastic in a casing and add an internal stay (in the manner of the gigot sleeve) to help keep the bottom edge of the sleeve in position without making its elastic excessively tight.

OFF-THE-SHOULDER SLEEVES

Off-the-shoulder sleeves are generally one of two types: either elastic-based (a piece of elastic is anchored to the front and back of the bodice and ornamented in some way) or fabric-based (a short or long sleeve, minus the upper part of the sleeve cap of the standard sleeve).

Elastic-Based Off-the-Shoulder Sleeves

Sometimes sleeves are simply an ornamented or fabric-covered elastic band anchored at the highest point of the armscye (Figure 3-63). To camouflage the elastic, use it as the base for

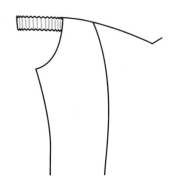

Figure 3-63: *This ³⁄₄-inch-wide elastic is anchored to the highest points of the front and back armscye; the elastic should be snug without being uncomfortable. Its job is to hold the bodice against the body at the shoulder area, and to support the sleeve.*

ornamentation, such as silk flowers, but be careful that the elastic isn't visible between the decorations when the wearer stretches the elastic as she moves her arm away from her body (Figures 3-64 and 3-65). You can also cover the elastic with a fabric casing that coordinates with the gown fabric. Avoid slippery fabrics for the casing, or the wearer will be continually pulling the elastic back toward her shoulder. Be sure the casing is long enough to cover the elastic when it is fully stretched.

Figure 3-64: *Here, silk flowers are anchored to a strong elastic base. Stitch the elastic in place, then you can determine the number of flowers needed, as well as their spacing, during a fitting.*

Figure 3-65: *These silk flowers hug the shoulder and cover the elastic amply, even when it is stretched.*

Fabric-Based Off-the-Shoulder Sleeves

LONG SLEEVES. A tightly fitted, off-the-shoulder sleeve presents a tricky fitting dilemma: how to maintain a slim, close-fitting sleeve silhouette while giving the wearer a reasonable range of arm motion. The width needed along the bicep line increases dramatically once the arm moves away from the body, but since the bodice is so tightly anchored to the torso, it allows for little movement. You can solve some of the dilemma by using a high, shallow armscye on both the sleeve and the bodice. Also, you can incorporate some of the extra width needed at the bicep line into small darts or encase it into subtle

elastic gathers along the top edge of the sleeve (Figure 3-66). Camouflage the darts or elastic with a three-dimensional fabric, such as Alençon lace, or another design detail, such as a row of hand-rolled silk roses, a single bow, or a number of bows.

SHORT SLEEVES. The movement considerations here are the same as for a long, off-the-shoulder sleeve. Finding a flattering length is a prime consideration, as is careful underlining. Although short, these sleeves must be substantial and well shaped (Figure 3-67). A short sleeve can also form a base for such treatments as ruching, pleats, or flowers.

Figure 3-67: *This guipure lace sleeve sits slightly away from the arm. In addition to internal stiffening, there is a separate piece of elastic in a silk casing.*

PUFF SLEEVES. These sleeves present no real problems other than coordinating fullness and proportion (Figure 3-68). The puff sleeve can overlay a sleeve stay, which gives a stable base to the

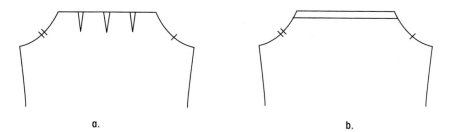

a.   b.

Figure 3-66: *Some of the extra fullness that is required across the bicep line can be eased into small darts along the top of the sleeve or it can be gathered into a casing for elastic.*

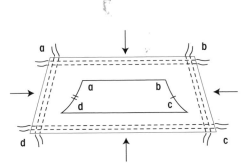

Figure 3-68: This puff sleeve will be so lofty, it will almost resemble meringue. The larger trapezoid-shaped piece of fashion fabric is gathered on all four sides, then stitched to the four edges of the smaller piece of underlining fabric. The smaller piece functions as a stay, or base, for the loftier, larger piece. Two rows of gathering, instead of the usual three, are sufficient; these gathers are full but easy to control.

underneath of the sleeve while maintaining the outward appearance of fullness and loft (Figure 3-69). Tack the topmost layer to the sleeve stay in one of these ways: Make easily hidden thread tacks, or incorporate single pearls, clusters of pearls, or tiny rosebuds into the tacks. If an underlying stay has not been used, incorporate inner ribbon stays in the manner of the upper part of a leg-of-mutton sleeve.

Figure 3-69: These exquisite puff sleeves are formed by gathering the topmost layer of silk (strengthened with a net underlining) on all four sides and securing it to a sleeve stay (which in this case resembles a band sleeve). The puffy topmost layer is tacked in place wherever desired.

Off-the-Shoulder Band Sleeves

Whether they're close to the body or away from it, whether used with elastic or not, band sleeves are derived from a portion of the standard sleeve (Figure 3-70a). These sleeves are not fully set into the armscye, so they are not as restricting as standard set-in sleeves. There are several ways to handle band sleeves: You can incorporate elastic into the top edge of the band (Figure 3-70b), or place it into its own casing. If the elastic is inde-

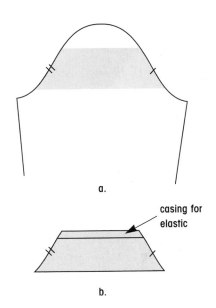

casing for elastic

b.

Figure 3-70: Cut the band sleeve from the portion of a standard sleeve above the bicep line and below the top of the sleeve cap (a). In addition to internal support to keep them upright and sturdy, band sleeves often have a casing for elastic along the top edge (b).

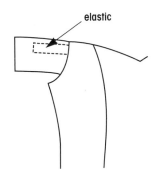

elastic

Figure 3-71: A band sleeve that curves around the upper arm without touching it must be rigid and yet maintain the shape of the band. In this case, the elastic is independent of the band sleeve.

pendent of the sleeve, the sleeve itself must have enough support to keep it from sagging (Figure 3-71). And if the band sleeve is to be positioned away from the arm—a very dramatic-looking application—the sleeve must have a sturdy underlining such as stiff netting or wide horsehair, singularly or in combination (Figure 3-72).

Figure 3-72: This dramatic band sleeve has stiff underlining to help it maintain its shape.

To give band sleeves a little extra ease, cut them on the bias, but be sure to underline them carefully so they don't give too much and loose their shape. Bias-cut bands will curve beautifully, and horsehair, added along the upper edge, will hold the curve in place and keep it from losing its shape.

SLEEVE SEAMS AND SEAM ALLOWANCES

Baste the sleeve seams first to check fit, correct if necessary, and then stitch. Use a narrow zigzag stitch for the seams of lace sleeves; the little bit of elasticity

Narrow zigzag

Figure 3-73: A narrow zigzag stitch offers a little bit of give to a lace seam.

the zigzag adds can be useful in a tight-fitting sleeve (Figure 3-73).

If the sleeve has a lining, simply carefully press and trim the seams. If the sleeve is long, straight, and tight-fitting, finish the lining at the hem with a small pleat. Then, baste the lining to the sleeve at the top edge, along the seamline. If the sleeve is full, there is usually little strain on the sleeve, so fell stitch the lining in place along the bottom edge without a pleat. Baste the layers together around the armscye, and, in the case of a gathered sleeve, gather the lining along with the fashion fabric.

If the sleeve is lace without an underlining, trim the seam allowances evenly, press them open, and catch stitch them in place (Figure 3-74). As

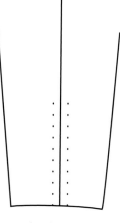

Figure 3-74: Catch stitches keep the seam allowances of a lace sleeve flat and in place. The stitches are fairly inconspicuous.

an alternative, treat the seam allowances as one and bind them with a bias strip of silk organza.

If the sleeve is lace with a silk organza underlining, treat the seam allowances the same way as those without an underlining. Alternatively, leave a wide seam allowance of silk organza on the undarted side, and use it to wrap around the other three trimmed seam allowances (Figure 3-75).

Figure 3-75: This lace and organza seam allowance is being wrapped with the organza seam allowance from the undarted side of the sleeve. It will encase the other three seam allowances. If all the seam allowances are narrowly trimmed, bind the seam allowance with a separate piece of organza.

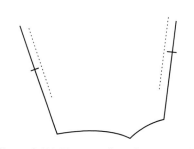

Figure 3-76: Using small stitches, reinforce the spot where the sleeves open. You may need to clip the seam later.

Two other excellent seam finishes include hand overcasting, the traditional couture seam finish, and a French seam. Use the French seam on sheer fabrics, but remember to reinforce the

opening on both sides before stitching the sleeve seam (Figure 3-76).

SLEEVE CLOSURES

The most straightforward sleeve is one that tapers enough to be visually narrow at the wrist but is just wide enough for the wearer to slip her hand in and out. An important consideration is finding the most flattering length, which is usually just below the wrist bone. Many brides, though, prefer the illusion of added length. Remember that the wearer's arm will often be bent (carrying a bouquet, dancing), having the effect of shortening the sleeve.

Zippers

Sleeve zippers, often used in couture, provide an inconspicuous closure (Figure 3-77). They needn't be longer than about four inches (cut a longer zipper to the length needed), and are easy to insert with a prick stitch. There is no great strain on sleeve zippers, but they must be evenly stitched on either side of the opening and line up perfectly at the hem. If the fabric is on the bias, or if the placket is at all off grain, stabilize the seam allowance from underneath with a strip of lightweight fabric, such as silk organza (Figure 3-78). Then, fell stitch the lining in place.

Figure 3-77: A hand-picked zipper is an efficient, easy-to-install sleeve closure. Carefully and neatly place the small stitches on the fashion fabric.

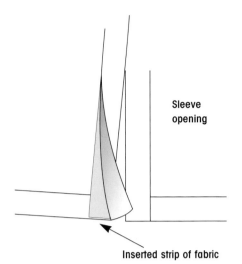

Figure 3-78: Openings in the base of the sleeve are often off grain, and the fabric used for sleeves can be less than sturdy. Insert an on-grain strip of fabric in the seam allowance to strengthen the area where the buttons or a zipper will be sewn.

Buttons and Loops

Buttons and loops are the standard bridal gown wrist closure. They are easy to apply, fun to wear, and since they are something we are unaccustomed to seeing, their presence is all the more special. Place the loops along the front edge of the opening and the buttons along the back edge. If there is a French seam or a bound seam, make a horizontal clip at the reinforced opening before applying the loops and finishing the seam allowances (Figure 3-79).

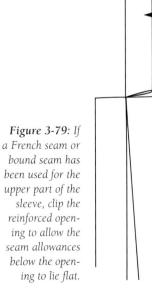

Figure 3-79: If a French seam or bound seam has been used for the upper part of the sleeve, clip the reinforced opening to allow the seam allowances below the opening to lie flat.

Apply commercially produced soutache bridal loops, available by the yard, to the front edge of the sleeve (the edge without the dart or ease) with the loop base at the seam allowance, and the loops themselves on the body of the sleeve (Figure 3-80a). Baste the loops in place along the seamline, making sure that the loops themselves are anchored all along the braid as well as at both ends. Leave an extra loop (or part of a loop) at either end to be secured after stitching is complete. Then, machine stitch the loops along the seamline (see Figure 3-80a). Sew another row of zigzag stitches along the braid to hold it in place along the seam allowance (Figure 3-80b). Tuck the extra loop at either end into the seam allowance. Fold along the seamline, flipping the loops into place along the edge (Figure 3-81). You can finish the seam allowance at the opening in a number of

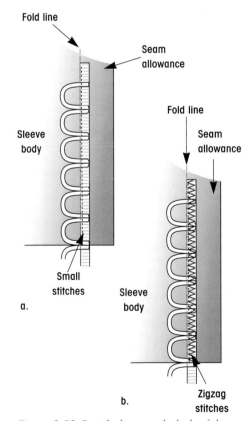

Figure 3-80: Rest the loops on the body of the sleeve, and the braid base on the seam allowance. Using small stitches, machine sew over the basting to straighten and anchor each loop. Then, add strength to the loops with a final row of zigzag stitches that will keep the braid base flat against the seam allowance.

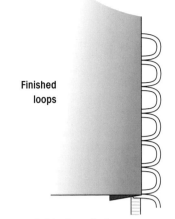

Figure 3-81: Once the loops are secured and the seam allowance is turned under, the loops stand out from the folded edge.

ways: Turn it under and tack it in place, neatly trim and hand overcast it, cover it with a small piece of narrow lace, or cover it with lining if there is an independent lining.

If the base on which the buttons are to be sewn is sheer, delicate, or on an unstable grain, insert a strip of organza under the seam allowance. A narrow piece of satin ribbon under the buttons on the inside of the sleeve can also serve as a base for the buttons (Figure 3-82). Then, sew the buttons on with double

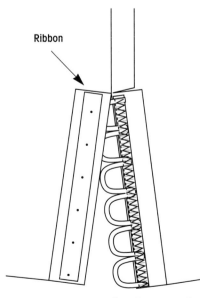

Figure 3-82: To strengthen the area underneath the buttons, slip a narrow piece of ribbon into the seam allowance. Not only does the ribbon serve to reinforce the fabric, but it eliminates stretching of an off-grain seam and keeps the buttons perfectly spaced.

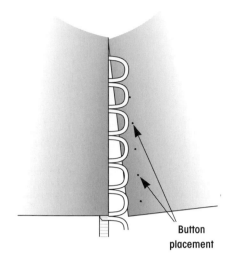

Figure 3-83: Sew the buttons in place slightly toward the body of the sleeve; the sleeve seams should abut, while the loops overlap the buttons.

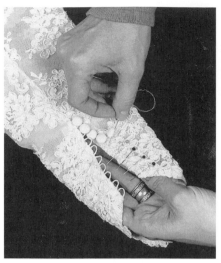

Figure 3-84: Buttons and loops must be placed carefully at the bottom of a sleeve; once buttoned, the edges of the sleeve opening should abut.

Figure 3-85: The edges of a cuff can abut, or there can be an overlap. A bias cuff will curve beautifully around the wrist; use underlining to keep it from stretching inappropriately.

thread coated with beeswax, just outside the seamline on the other side of the closure (Figures 3-83 and 3-84). Although there is no overlap of fabric and no placket, the loops overlap just enough for the edges to abut once the buttons are sewn in place and buttoned.

If you're using self-made loops, be sure that they are all exactly the same circumference and length. Then, sew them in place the same way you would apply commercial versions.

Cuffs

Often a sheer sleeve ends in a cuff—it can be narrow or wide, on the straight of grain or on the bias, in the same fabric as the rest of the sleeve or in something contrasting. Buttons can appear solely on the cuff, or they can extend up onto the sleeve. Loops can be purchased, self-made, or made from reinforced thread bars. The placket opening can be narrowly hemmed, or in the case of a chiffon sleeve, can be hand rolled. The cuff can overlap, or the edges can abut (Figure 3-85). If the overlap is significant, put a small snap on the underlap to help keep it in place, or use a large, decorative button to camouflage it. The buttons can really button, or the cuff can fasten with silk-covered snaps (Figure 3-86).

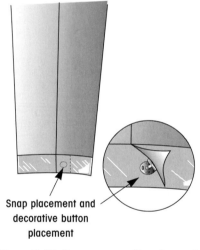

Snap placement and decorative button placement

Figure 3-86: Buttons on a cuff can be purely decorative; silk-covered snaps can do the actual closing. If there is a sizeable overlap, use two snaps to prevent shifting of the layers.

The Skirt

Nothing conveys the feel of the gown more than the skirt. Our first impression of the bride comes as she walks down the aisle, the skirt flowing gracefully behind her.

Acting on its own or serving as a luxurious background for lace or other design elements, the sheer amount of fabric in the skirt is often enough to lend magnificence to the picture. The upper part of the gown, at least initially, is usually obscured by a veil and a bouquet of flowers, so it is the skirt—its fabrication, its proportions, its movement, the sound of the fabric rustling as the bride walks past, that speaks to us. And although the fabrication and stylistic elements do the communicating, it is the inner details and the underlining that do the critical work behind the scenes.

The most common bridal skirt shape is one which is gathered at or below the natural waist, widens into a full skirt, and lengthens in the back to form a train. The circumference is usually not less than six yards. In order to avoid a center front seam and to accommodate the width needed at the bottom of the skirt panels (especially at the back), there are usually seven panels: a center front panel, two side front panels, two side back panels, and two center back panels (Figure 3-87). There is almost always a center back seam. The extra length needed for the train usually begins at the side seams and slopes back to the base of the center back seam. Wedding gown skirt lengths vary from mini-skirt length to cathedral length. Variations in length depend upon the bride's height, the weight of the fashion fabric, the setting in which the gown will be worn, whether the train will later be detached, and the bride's preference.

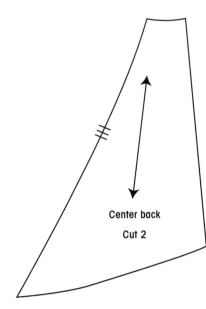

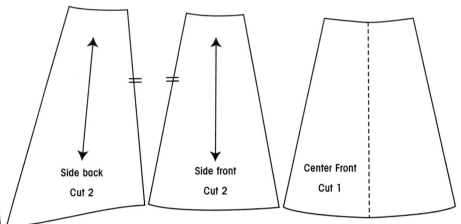

Figure 3-87: These are the seven panels used in most bridal skirts: the center front (there is rarely a center front seam), two side front panels, two side back panels, and the two center back panels. Extra length usually begins at the side seams.

SKIRT CONSTRUCTION

Here are guidelines for constructing the skirt of a gown. Adapt the information to your chosen gown design.

Lay Out and Cut the Skirt

Before laying out the skirt, carefully determine its length. You can do this during a fitting in which the bride is wearing a fully ironed-out crinoline (separate from the skirt) as well as heels of the height she will eventually wear with the gown. Allow extra length beyond a sufficient hem, if possible.

Matching skirt seams have the same slope (the same angle of grain), so any alterations in width made to one skirt panel must also be made to the corresponding skirt panel; otherwise, the hang of the skirt will be affected adversely. As long as nap is not a factor, the center back and side back pieces are usually placed together as they are the longest pieces and their matching angles of grain make it possible to abut corresponding seams (in this case, the side back seams). Cut the center front in a single layer, avoiding a crease along the center front (Figure 3-88). Some satins have a nap; shantung and douppioni do not.

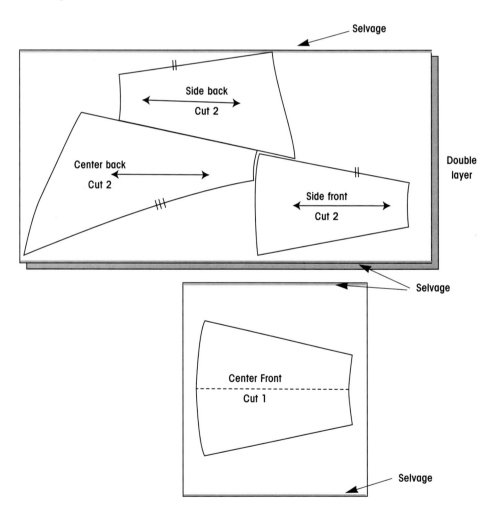

Figure 3-88: If a nap layout isn't necessary, place the side back panels and the center back panels next to each other; their adjoining seams have the same degree of slope, so they can abut. Cut the front panel in a single layer to avoid a crease down the center front.

If a little extra length is needed, add it to the top edges of the skirt panels instead of the bottom edges (Figure 3-89). Adding to the top will narrow the

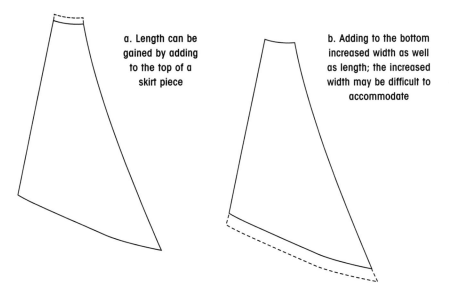

a. Length can be gained by adding to the top of a skirt piece

b. Adding to the bottom increased width as well as length; the increased width may be difficult to accommodate

Figure 3-89: You can make small adjustments in length to the top of the pattern pieces (a) as well as to the bottom (b), to save fabric.

Figure 3-90: This six-yard length of cutwork-bordered linen is simply seamed at the center back (patterns are carefully matched up and the seam allowance is hand overcast), hemmed, and gathered.

skirt incrementally, but it is a good alternative when additional length cannot easily be accommodated at the bottom edges without piecing.

If the skirt will use a bordered fabric—popular in ankle-length gowns—predetermine the exact skirt length (Figure 3-90). In ankle-length gowns, the constant skirt length eliminates the problem of curving the border (which a train would necessitate). In any event, the width of a bordered fabric (usually 45 inches) isn't sufficient to allow for much of a train. The border itself, however, could be removed and re-applied around a longer, curved hem.

Take extraordinary care that the front panel is free of marks, imperfections, or fold lines. It isn't a bad idea to have extra material, at least for the center front panel, just in case. Be careful to place pins in the seam allowances, especially with satin, peau de soie, taffeta, and moiré.

After cutting the fashion fabric and underlining, place markings on the underlining. Then, stabilize all top edges with a zigzag stitch. In addition, stabilize the front panels along the bottom edges, which are on somewhat of a straight grain. If there is a train, there will be enough of an angle along the bottom edges of the four back panels so that stabilizing isn't necessary.

Attach the Underlining

Although never seen on the finished garment, the underlining (sometimes referred to as the backing) plays a critical role in the skirt's success. After the underlining has been carefully marked, baste it to the fashion fabric and treat the two as one thereafter. Underlining adds strength to the fashion fabric, and in so doing, adds shape to the garment, filling out pleats and gathers, padding seams, and strengthening the base on which lace and other embellishments will be applied. It also allows the garment to be hemmed invisibly (stitches are applied to the underlining, not the fashion fabric), lessens wrinkling, and prevents stretching and bagging.

Choose underlining with care; it is one of your biggest allies in the process of creating the perfect gown. For example, silk organza will add crisp, lightweight support, cotton batiste will add soft support, poly-cotton batiste will be too thick and heavy for most skirts. Good choices for skirt underlinings include: silk organza—a stable, lightweight yet firm fabric that is often a couturier's favorite; cotton batiste—a fabric that lends a softness to the skirt, yet has enough weight to add swing; self-fabric—a luxurious choice which guarantees compatibility with the fashion fabric (crepes and crepe de chine are often underlined with self-fabric); and cotton voile—a soft, light underlining that adds just a whisper of weight and grace to the fashion fabric.

Cut the underlining exactly the same as the fashion fabric. The lower, outer corners of the longer panels can be pieced discreetly, if necessary. Silk organza, for example, is often 42 inches wide, so rather than increase the yardage dramatically to match panels that have been laid out on 45-inch-wide fashion fabric, piece the organza panels carefully. During pressing, take care that the pieced seams and seam allowances of the underlining don't show through the fashion fabric.

After cutting and marking the underlining (and zigzagging any edges that are likely to ravel), join the fashion fabric and the underlining by hand. Spread the layers out, checking to make sure that grain is consistent and that there are no threads or bits of fluff inside the layers. Adjust the bottom edge after handling, pressing, and allowing the skirt to hang out, but join each panel on all four sides initially. Secure the layers with large basting stitches.

Sew and Finish the Skirt Seams

Sew skirt seams in a straightforward manner from the bottom up (so that the pieces narrow). First, baste the seams together to keep the layers from shifting (there will be four layers: two of fashion fabric, two of underlining). Then, do the permanent stitching. After stitching, remove the basting from the stitched seams (without disturbing the

basting around the top edge, the hemline, or the back opening). Press the seams while unopened to meld the stitches. Then open the seams (your fingernail does this perfectly) and press them open.

A successful seam finish will keep material from fraying, and leave no ridge or mark on the fashion fabric. If a skirt will be completely lined, and the lining will join at the hem, then careful trimming and pressing may suffice. The seams will not be abraded, so there probably won't be serious fraying. Remember, that nearly all (if not all) of the skirt seams of a traditional full skirt are off grain, lessening or nearly eliminating their tendency to ravel.

Trim the seams before or after pressing. Serrated shears will do the best job, especially if the fabric is slippery. Once the skirt has been put together, place a row of staystitching around the top of the skirt (be sure that seam allowances are open) to join the layers securely. If there is a V at the center front, use shorter stitches on either side of the V. Add a small square of silk organza at the V for reinforcement beyond that given by the underlining (Figure 3-91).

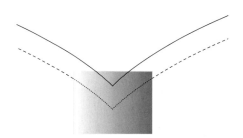

Figure 3-91: *To reinforce the V at the center front of the skirt, add a small piece of silk organza. Use shorter stitches near the center.*

If the inside of the skirt will not be covered with a lining, the optimal couture seam finish is trimming and hand overcasting. One variation of hand overcasting involves a narrow row of stitching close to the edge, stitched in the same direction in which the skirt was stitched (Figure 3-92). Hand overcasting is then done in the narrow channel between the row of stitching and the edge of the fabric. Another variation is a narrow zigzag, stitched in the

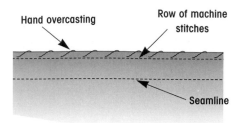

Figure 3-92: *Hand overcasting is a beautiful seam finish for long, straight skirt seams; a row of stitching, close to the edge, is sometimes added to edges that are particularly likely to fray.*

direction the seam was stitched to minimize distortion.

French seams are an option for sheer fabrics, but keep in mind that they are more successful if the seams are on the straight of grain. Otherwise, be sure that the seam allowances lie perfectly flat after having been stitched the second time (off-grain French seams can develop drag lines).

Gather the Skirt

Experimentation will tell you the proper gathering stitch length (stitches should be as small as possible) while allowing reasonably easy gathering, especially over bulky seams. Use three rows of stitches: one on the seamline, and two within the seam allowance. After gathering, work the gathers back and forth until all three rows of thread are pulled with the same tension and until the gathers are lined up like tiny cartridge pleats (Figure 3-93). Once the

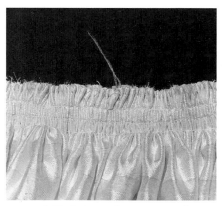

Figure 3-93: *Before gathering, zigzag the top edges to discourage raveling while the gathers are worked back and forth. Pull all three rows of thread evenly, and line the gathers up vertically.*

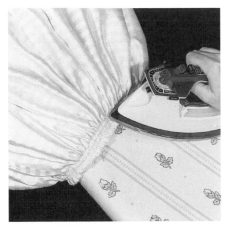

Figure 3-94: Press the seam allowance to reduce bulk and to encourage the gathers to stay in place.

gathers are properly spaced, press the seam allowance flat (Figure 3-94); pressing cuts down on bulk and encourages the "pleats" to stay in place until stitched.

For a skirt with a V at the center front, you'll need two independent sets of gathers from center front to center back. Once these gathers are in place, secure the gathering stitches. Pull both threads to the inside and knot them. For a skirt with a V, there will be six sets of knots at the center front (Figure 3-95). There is usually little gathering right at the center front (and often little on the entire center front panel), but the center of the front panel serves as a good anchor point for the threads, even if the gathers themselves start some distance out from the actual center.

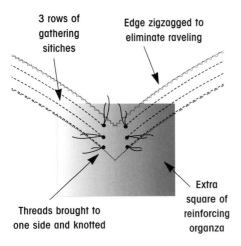

Figure 3-95: Pull the ends of the gathering threads to one side, then knot each pair of threads.

If there is a lining, gather it at the same time that the skirt is gathered, treating the fashion fabric, the underlining and the lining as one. Work the center back closure out in advance, however, as the lining and the fashion fabric are likely to be treated differently there. Otherwise, gather the lining separately and sew it in place later by hand or machine. For reduced bulk at the waistline, pleat the lining instead of gathering it.

Stitch Any Pleats

Skirts can be pleated, for a more gradual transition from the tightness of the bodice to the fullness of the skirt. The leading edges of the pleats can face either inward or outward, although one side usually mirrors the other starting at the center front. Stitch the pleats securely in place by hand in the seam allowance to prevent them from shifting while they are being sewn to the bodice (Figure 3-96). Lining up pleats evenly and symmetrically takes time. Place pins only in the seam allowances; lining up pleats can be tedious, and the pinning and re-pinning may damage the fabric. The underlining, which will encourage the pleats to form nicely and stay in place, will also combat excess wrinkling.

Hem the Skirt

The primary role of the hem is to finish off the bottom edge of the gown, and its most important task is to do this inconspicuously (unless there is a purposely placed fashion detail along the hem). Underlining is the dressmaker's biggest ally when hemming: the hem is sewn to the underlining, not to the fashion fabric. The lining must also be considered, as discussed on pages 83–84.

Bridal skirts are usually hemmed from ¾ to 1½ inches off the floor at the center front. Closer to the floor than ¾ inch is too much of a liability; higher than 1½ inches can look too short. The distance off the floor is consistent up to the side seams, at which point the skirt begins lengthening to form the train.

The basting stitches that join the fashion fabric to the underlining may need to be restitched after realigning the layers, as small discrepancies are likely to have occurred as a result of cutting, pressing, and the varying weights of the layers. Once the two layers are properly aligned, hold them together permanently with a loose basting stitch along the fold line (Figure 3-97). Couture hems are never pressed flat (with the possible exception of linen or narrowly-hemmed chiffon);

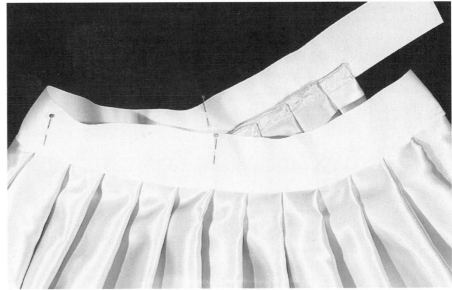

Figure 3-96: These pleats are from a pleated skirt, and therefore fall from the natural waist. They have been thoroughly tacked, after which they were anchored to a waistline stay, which will later be covered by a waistband.

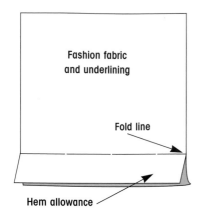

Figure 3-97: *To prepare for hemming, baste the underlining and the fashion fabric together at the fold line. Keep the stitches loose, allowing only the tiniest amount of thread showing through to the right side.*

instead, they are gently folded into place, and sometimes even padded to emphasize the soft fold.

STRAIGHT SKIRT HEMS

For a sheath skirt or other hem in which there is little or no excess circumference to be incorporated, there are several hemming options. Before stitching, always stabilize the hem with a row of basting stitches between the fold line and the top of the hem allowance (Figure 3-98).

- Hand overcast, turn up, and invisibly hem the bottom edge (Figure 3-99).
- Sew lace seam binding by hand or machine to the bottom edge, and then turn it up and invisibly hem it (Figure 3-100).
- Catch stitch the hem in place and then cover it with the lining (Figure 3-101).
- Invisibly stitch a heavy hem twice (Figure 3-102).
- Bind the seam allowance with a Hong Kong finish, turn it up, and invisibly hem it (Figure 3-103).

- Stiffen the hem with horsehair of various widths, from narrow—to lend subtle definition—to wide—to encourage a dramatically shaped hem to stay somewhat stiffly in place (Figure 3-104).
- Pad the hem to soften the folded edge (Figure 3-105).
- Weight the hem either with encased lead weights or with a narrow tube of lead pellets; in either case, camouflage their presence (Figure 3-106).

Although it is always tempting to anchor hem stitches at the vertical seamlines, be careful that this doesn't distort the straight, clean line of the hem. There is more upward tension at the seams than in the body of the fabric, and anchoring stitches there can subtly pull up the hem and spoil the line.

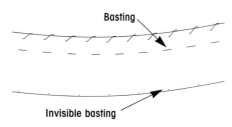

Figure 3-98: *Use a row of basting stitches to hold the hem in place as it is stitched.*

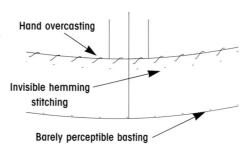

Figure 3-99: *A hand-overcast edge, which is invisibly hemmed, will leave little or no impression on the fashion fabric.*

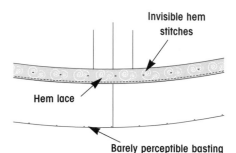

Figure 3-100: *Attach the narrow hem lace by hand or machine; then hem the skirt invisibly.*

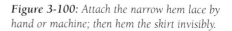
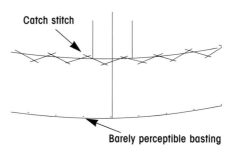

Figure 3-101: *Distribute the weight of a heavy hem with a catch stitch.*

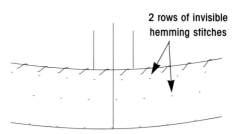

Figure 3-102: *Use two rows of invisible stitching on particularly heavy hems; the hem allowance will be controlled and its weight will be distributed.*

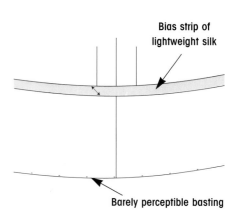

Figure 3-103: *A Hong Kong finish is beautiful and clean and works well as long as there is no ridge visible on the fashion fabric side.*

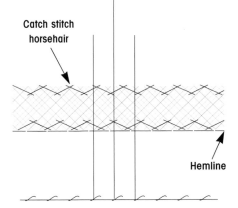

Figure 3-104: Horsehair can be an invaluable addition to hems; a wide piece of horsehair shapes a hem beautifully. Catch stitch it in place to the underlining before the hem is stitched. Overlap and cover its ends to prevent its stiff fibers from working their way through the fabric layers.

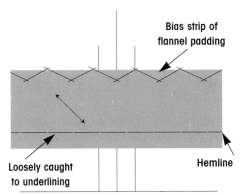

Figure 3-105: Hems in couture are seldom, if ever, pressed flat to form a knife-like edge; rather, they are gently folded, and often even padded, for a soft effect. The padding lies to either side of the hem fold; catch stitch it in place.

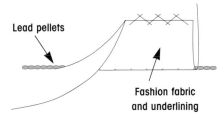

Figure 3-106: Lead weights help hold the skirt in line; use individual weights in specific areas, or place a strip of lead pellets inside the hem. If the underlining and fashion fabric aren't sufficient camouflage, then add padding along the fold line.

FULL-SKIRT HEMS

In the case of a full skirt, the circumference of the bottom edge of the skirt will be much greater than the circumference of the skirt where it will be stitched. Therefore, the extra bulk must be dealt with. Here are some options:

- Hand-roll or carefully machine stitch a narrow hem. This eliminates the discrepancy in circumference.
- Ease the fullness into hem lace by stretching the lace as it is sewn. As the lace relaxes, it, in effect, gathers the fashion fabric. Experimentation will show the correct amount of stretch.
- Use wide horsehair that has a built-in gathering thread. This will allow the horsehair to be wide at the hem line, and narrow as the skirt circumference narrows (Figure 3-107).
- Notch the hem or slit it and overlap it.
- Pleat the excess fullness or create darts (Figure 3-108).

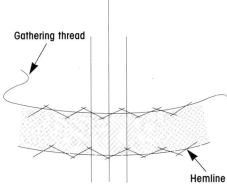

Figure 3-107: If horsehair is used in a hem in which there is excess fullness, gather it along its top edge (wide horsehair has a gathering thread along one edge) so it takes on the contour of the hem. Otherwise, the hem will flare instead of lying flat. Baste or catch stitch it in place, overlapping the ends to make sure no sharp fibers work their way through the fabric layers.

- Baste the hem in place before stitching, somewhere between the fold of the fabric and the stitching line, in order to stabilize the hem allowance and to distribute its weight and fullness evenly.

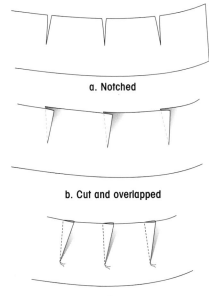

a. Notched

b. Cut and overlapped

c. Darts

Figure 3-108: The excess fullness in the hem can be dealt in several ways: notch it (a), slit and overlap it (b), or create darts (c).

Attach the Skirt Lining

Lining requirements vary. Depending on the fabrication and the underlining, the skirt may not need to be lined. A wedding gown skirt with a long, full train could be of silk shantung underlined with silk organza; the silk organza acts somewhat as a lining. If worn with a full crinoline (as most wedding gown skirts are), a lining isn't necessary for the purposes of modesty, and as long as seams are well finished and the skirt is securely and attractively hemmed, there is no inner structure to cover up.

In the case of a full skirt, determine the lining treatment before gathering the skirt. If there is to be a full lining in the skirt, gather it along with the skirt. If this is too bulky (and it may be, depending on the fashion fabric and the underlining), then gather the skirt lining independently, or, to reduce bulk, pleat it. If the lining will be treated separately at the top, then tack it into place after the skirt has been sewn to the bodice.

The lining can float free at the hem, join the skirt hem intermittently with French tacks, be hemmed along with the skirt, or be attached to the hemline after the fashion fabric has been hemmed. Here are considerations for each option.

FREE-FLOATING LINING

There are times when the lining can help add loft and flare to a skirt, and there are times when the skirt and lining are most effective independent of one another. A chiffon skirt is the most obvious example. An independent lining can be hemmed narrowly by machine, and the lightweight nature of the lining will be maintained. There are times, though, when a more substantial lining hem (deeper or reinforced with horsehair) is a better choice. The additional weight and structure along the hem of the lining will allow it to provide a firmer base for whatever is floating over it, giving it a structural, as well as cosmetic, role.

An underlined skirt with a train can have an independent ankle-length lining. However, there must be no visual discrepancy at the point at which the lining stops but the skirt does not (Figure 3-109). Some fabrics will show the discrepancy, and some will not.

LINING JOINED TO THE SKIRT WITH FRENCH TACKS

An independent lining sometimes becomes too independent of the skirt that it lines, shifting out of position and becoming uneven and ineffective. The perfect way to keep the layers together without joining the hemlines completely is to use French tacks (also called swing tacks). Treat the fashion fabric and underlining as one, and hem them to the underlining. Join the hems of the skirt and lining intermittently with

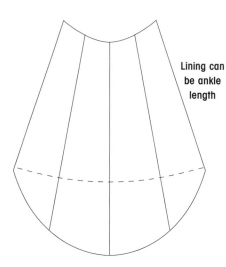

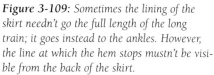

Figure 3-109: Sometimes the lining of the skirt needn't go the full length of the long train; it goes instead to the ankles. However, the line at which the hem stops mustn't be visible from the back of the skirt.

thread chains (Figure 3-110). The chain can vary in length, but is often an inch or so long. Sometimes, the tacks are necessary only in the back of the dress (if there is a short train, for example) or at the sides. With fairly well-behaved layers, only a few tacks may be needed; with something more unruly, more will be necessary.

French tacks are also useful for those times when, although cut from the

same pattern, the fashion fabric and the lining are impossible to align. Rather than distort the skirt by trying to line up the layers, leave the lining separate, but keep it in place with thread tacks.

LINING AND SKIRT HEMMED TOGETHER

There are times when the fashion fabric and the lining are joined at the hem. In this case, treat the lining much like the underlining: Baste all the layers together loosely along the fold line, allowing only the tiniest bit of thread to show on the fashion fabric side. turn up the hem and stitch in the usual manner. The entire hem will be visible, so it must be cleanly and elegantly finished off. Use hem lace or a Hong Kong finish.

LINING OVERHANGING THE SKIRT HEM

If the skirt, lining, and underlining are all long, the lining can be attached in the traditional manner: The skirt and underlining are hemmed together, then the lining is sewn in place over the joined layers with a pleat. It is critical to have this overhang, especially if the garment is tight fitting. The edge of the lining needn't be sharply pressed; it can be folded in place and smoothed by hand.

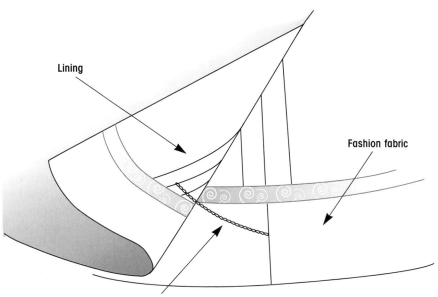

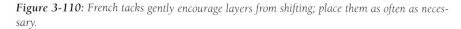

Figure 3-110: French tacks gently encourage layers from shifting; place them as often as necessary.

SKIRT STYLES

Here are some descriptions and construction considerations for a variety of skirt styles.

Peplums and Overlays

Peplums and overlays can be short or long, fitted, gathered, graduated, all the way around, or just in the back (Figure 3-111). They will have more loft if the peplum, or overlay, is gathered independently of the skirt, then joined. You can hide their center back opening in a gather or a fold, or you can make the opening part of the design. You can narrowly hem peplums, self-face them, or line them for contrast. To give them a prominent hemline, use horsehair or piping; the hem edge will become more important, design-wise, as more flare is built in. If you join peplum layers along their lower edge (as with a peplum which is completely faced, for example), you may have to realign their top edges; there is likely to be some shifting, especially if part of the peplum is on the bias.

Figure 3-111: These small layered peplums are lined in pink and appliquéd with Alençon lace. They are gathered along with the skirt; the extra loft created by separately gathered layers isn't desirable in this instance.

Multilayered Skirts

Multilayered skirts can have a top layer that is fuller than the underlayers, especially if the top layer is transparent or semi-transparent. You can gather the various layers at the same time if they have the same circumference along the top edge, or you can gather them separately to add more loft. Hem the top layer very slightly longer than the underlayer(s) to make sure the underlayer doesn't peek through at the hem.

Multilayered skirts can achieve wonderful effects with colors, from the subtle to the strong, especially with top layers of chiffon, mousseline, or organza. Be aware, though, that they need special seam treatment if the top layer is sheer. French seams are an option, if seams aren't prominent, prominently placed, or stiff. Other choices include finishing standard seams with hand overcasting or wrapping the seam allowances in neutral-colored silk organza or chiffon.

Tiered Skirts

Tiered skirts need a firm base on which to attach the tiers, and they must accommodate extra length at the back if the skirt has a train. To accommodate extra length, you must create more tiers at the back than at the front, or you must make the tiers longer toward the back.

When planning the skirt, map out the placement of the tiers on the skirt base, and be sure to calculate the amount of overlap of the tiers, as well. Mark the stitching lines with basting or staystitching (Figure 3-112).

You can cut and gather the tiers themselves on the straight of grain or the bias. The tiers can be hemmed in a number of ways. Hem the fabric before gathering it, or fold it so that the fashion fabric is doubled and hemming isn't necessary. If the fabric is cut on the bias, you may not need to finish the gathered edge. If the fabric needs to be hemmed, consider how the type of hem will affect the look of the gathers. For greatest loft,

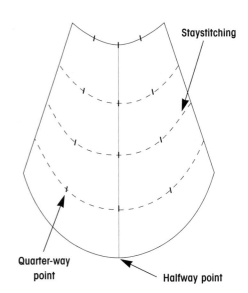

Figure 3-112: Mark placement lines for tiers on the base fabric; then hand or machine baste the lines. Then, mark halfway and quarter-way points help place the tiers evenly.

stitch the ruffles so that the seam allowances go down instead of up.

Skirts with Graduated Hemlines

Skirts with graduated hemlines taper from a high point (usually the center front, but it can be the side front or even at the side) to a low point (usually the center back). These skirts must be lined so that seam allowances aren't visible, regardless of the angle from which the skirt is seen.

Skirts with Built-In Bustles

A built-in bustle is layered on top of a stay, an underlayer that is flat and that prevents the bustle from going anywhere (Figures 3-113 and 3-114). When planning a bustle, carefully consider its underlining(s); net will add strength without weight. In addition, you may need to fill the bustle with tulle to help maintain its shape. Camouflage the bustle's center back opening in gathers or a fold, or with flowers.

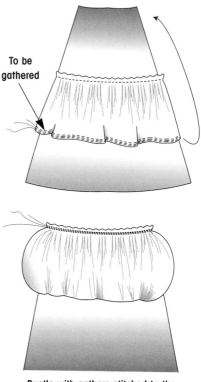

**Bustle with gathers stitched to the
top of the skirt**

Figure 3-114: A built-in bustle has been placed over a flat layer of fabric, which functions as a stay. After sewing the bustle's bottom edge, fold it up and join it to the top of the skirt. The sides will be stitched later.

Skirts with a Circular Ruffle

The distance from the center of the circle to the top edge of the ruffle will determine its fullness. The further the top edge of the ruffle is from the center point of the circle, the less full the ruffle will be (Figure 3-115). Join sections along the straight of grain, not along the bias. Staystitch along its inner edge to prevent stretching, and then gather the ruffle slightly with one of the staystitching threads if ease is required. Zigzag stitch along the top edge to prevent ravelling.

Figure 3-113: A flat skirt panel, under the bustle, is what allows the bustle to maintain its shape. The bustle itself is gathered along both its top and bottom edges and, to increase loft, is filled with soft tulle.

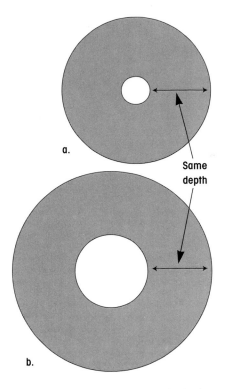

Figure 3-115: Although the same depth, these two ruffles will differ in fullness and effect. Ruffle a will be fuller than ruffle b. Its circumference is smaller, though, so it will cover less distance than ruffle b.

Figure 3-116: Three rows of bias-cut silk douppioni have been shaped around the curve of the hem. They have been staystitched, basted, and then slip stitched.

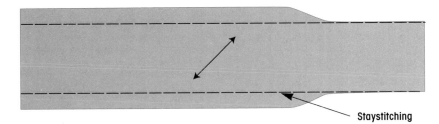

Figure 3-117: Bias strips require gentle handling: staystitch them, then press them carefully on the stitching line to prepare them for slip stitching onto the fashion fabric. Machine sewing is too risky; the strips are likely to stretch, compromising a beautiful result.

Skirts with Bias Strips at the Hem

Bias-cut strips are perfect for accommodating the curves of a skirt (Figure 3-116). Join bias strips on the straight of grain and match them carefully; certain fabrics (especially douppioni) piece imperceptibly, if pieced on the crosswise grain. To make them easy to control, staystitch the strips along the fold line (Figure 3-117). Be sure to shape them before applying them by hand with a slip stitch and handle them as little as possible. When placing them on the skirt, follow a staystitched or basted line and position the strips so that joins in the strips are located inconspicuously. Press bias strips carefully to avoid ripples.

Tulle Skirts

Tulle creates a nicely full skirt if you use six or seven layers, on top of a fashion fabric underskirt. Tulle is available in widths of up to 108 inches, and sometimes even 144 inches; the wider the tulle, the more likely the skirt can be cut without seams or with only a center back seam. Tulle is very flattering when cut to ankle length; the chances of this delicate fabric being stepped on are little. Tulle makes an attractive small-sweep train, although backward movement, as is needed for dancing, can be awkward. A tulle skirt can be shaded with color; for example, pastel tulle can be hidden several layers down for a subtle hint of color.

Cut all layers for a tulle skirt at once, and then hand baste the layers around the top edge even before moving them from the cutting surface. Cut the layers to the proper length around the bottom edge, so that little, if any, further trimming will be needed to finish the hemline. If the hemline needs adjusting, trim one layer at a time, starting with the bottom-most layer. Tulle skirts can be also be trimmed with a narrow ribbon along the hemline; in order for the ribbon to lie absolutely flat, the ribbon must be stitched twice, once along each edge, in the same direction (Figure 3-118). Before sewing, make sure that the ribbon is long enough to go around the skirt without being joined more than once. The ribbon should be stitched close to, although not along, the edge of the tulle. Trim the excess tulle later.

When gathering a tulle skirt, gather all the layers at once; they can be pulled apart later at the waist if extra fullness is desired. Stabilize the center back seam opening along the fold line to lessen the possibility of tearing.

Other options for tulle include decorating it with sequins, pearls, or rhinestones, which can be applied to the topmost layer, or, for a more subtle effect, to the second layer. It can also be bustled, but the layers can look puffy rather than gracefully drawn up into a bustle.

Skirts with a Gathered-Up Overlay

A gathered overlay is formed by an overskirt that is pulled up, or gathered vertically, at intervals (Figure 3-119). The overlay can be embellished with bows or flowers at the points where the overlay is drawn up.

Carefully determine proportions at the muslin stage. You'll need to consider how often to gather, how far up the gathers should be pulled, and how full the overlay should be. Overlays can vary in length and shape, and they can be separate at the center front.

Skirts with Variable Fullness

A skirt has variable fullness if one part of the skirt is fuller than another. Sometimes the back is more gathered, and sometimes extra support is built in from underneath. Internal stays, such as twill tape or ribbon, keep the fullness anchored in a particular area and keep it from spreading (Figure 3-120).

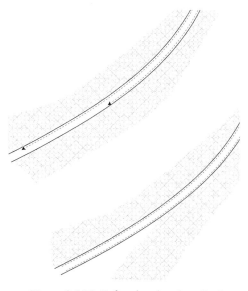

Figure 3-118: *Define the edge of a tulle skirt beautifully with narrow ribbon; stitch the ribbon twice in the same direction, just inside either edge of the ribbon. Then, cut away the excess tulle after stitching.*

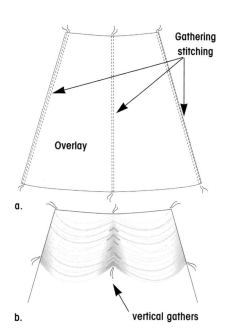

Figure 3-119: *The overskirt should be fuller than the underskirt in order to drape properly; work out the proportions in muslin.*

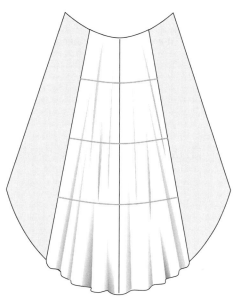

Figure 3-120: *Internal stays can concentrate fullness in a specific area of a skirt; use them to keep the fullness from shifting to unwanted areas.*

Joining the Gown's Components

After all the work of boning, underlining, endless hand stitching, and careful attention to fit, the fun begins as the major sections are sewn together and the dress really starts to take shape.

JOINING THE BODICE AND THE SLEEVES

The sleeves and bodice are usually not overly cumbersome to join, nor overly difficult. Putting in the sleeves is a very straightforward process, and the pleasure of the job is enhanced by the excitement of having arrived at this fairly advanced stage of the gown process.

Add Any Linings

Before the bodice and sleeves are joined, they need to be lined. Unlike some linings, which are assembled in their entirety and then inserted into a garment, the bodice and sleeve linings are put in beforehand and separately. Sleeves are often lined as a step in their construction process, and the bodice is lined after its final fitting. In both cases, the linings are basted at the armscyes, which both secures them to the garment section and serves as a stitching guideline.

Trim the Seam Allowances

Once fit has been assured, trim the bodice and sleeve seam allowances at the armscye; a seam allowance of ½ inch or so should be adequate; wider than that will create unnecessary bulk, and narrower might not be secure enough, especially if there is a lot of pull on the armscye (Figure 3-121). Trim inner bulk out of the seam

allowances (extra pieces of lace, pearls and sequins, and net). If horsehair has been used to stiffen the top edge of an off-the-shoulder sleeve, it needs to be trimmed; it must remain caught in the stitching line to be effective, but

Figure 3-121: Trim the armscye seam allowances of both the bodice and the sleeves before stitching them together.

beyond that, it should be trimmed. Its sharp edges will eventually work their way through the seam binding if they are not shortened.

Sew the Sleeves to the Bodice

First, baste the units together, taking great care to line up motifs, design details, and edges. Basting also ensures that the side seam and the underarm seam line up perfectly. Next, hand stitch seams that are too bulky to be sewn by machine. Sew them with double thread that has been coated with beeswax. A back stitch works well; this is not a seam which will be pressed open, so hand stitches, if carefully done, will never be seen. There are times when forcing a huge sleeve into a small armscye on the machine would compromise accuracy. Further, it might damage the fabric, and it might put in wrinkles that would be impossible to remove.

When machine sewing, change to a thicker machine needle to accommodate all the layers involved. Sleeves can also be partially sewn by hand, partial-

ly by machine. A thick, tightly gathered sleeve head may be too thick to sew on by machine, but the lower armscye can be machine stitched. It is critical that the width of the shoulder seam be consistent on the two sides; sometimes the control possible with hand stitching will guarantee a more exact result. Once the sleeve has been stitched and checked for correct placement, remove the basting stitches.

Insert Elastic

If an independent piece of elastic is used in an off-the-shoulder sleeve, encase the elastic in fabric (a piece of lining fabric is fine) or leave it uncovered. Although not as attractive if left uncovered, elastic does grip better; silk-covered elastic is slippery. Consider color; if, for example, a piece of elastic were needed for the top of a black lace sleeve, it wouldn't make sense to cover the elastic with black silk; in this case, an organza casing that matched the wearer's skin tone would serve as a good camouflage for the elastic.

Stretch the elastic when measuring it for the casing; the elastic will be stretched while the gown is being worn, so the casing must accommodate the extra length. Establish the length of the elastic during fittings, remembering that its length can vary from one side of the body to the other. The tightness of the elastic has to do with engineering, but it also has to do with the wearer's comfort. Too tight, and the elastic will have a tendency to pull the sleeve down; too loose, and it's useless. It must be both snug and reasonably comfortable. Sew the sleeve in first, then the elastic; position the elastic carefully. The angle of the elastic is sometimes different from that of the top of the sleeve; the elastic goes out at a right angle, whereas the top of the sleeve may angle up toward the "corner" of the shoulder (Figure 3-122).

Add Gussets if Needed

Gussets are a wonderful way to give a little extra movement to a tight-fitting

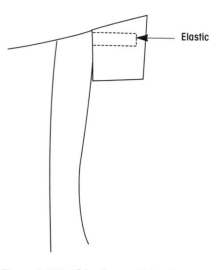

Figure 3-122: If the sleeve and the elastic are independent of one another, the angles at which they are stitched in place can differ.

armscye. What they do is allow the armscye to be opened up at the underarm, with the gusset forming a patch over the opening. Gussets cannot make up for ill-fitting sleeves, nor can they create an enormous range of motion, but they can allow some extra movement by extending the side-seam and underarm-seam length.

Gauge the best placement and size for a gusset during a fitting. Baste both sleeves on the bodice, and if there is enough pulling to warrant inserting gussets, open the seam at the underarm. The seam will open up, mimicking the shape of the gusset. Gussets are usually either diamond-shaped or football-shaped. The opening will often extend several inches to either side of the center of the underarm. When the wearer's arm is down, though, the gusset folds itself in half quite inconspicuously.

Cut gussets on the bias; make a pattern by placing a small piece of silk organza over the opening and pinning it in place. Then trace the outline of the opening. Use the organza as a pattern. Gussets should match the fabrication of the bodice and sleeves (if they are different, choose the fabrication of one or the other). Pin the gussets in place; then stitch them by machine or with a fell stitch (Figure 3-123).

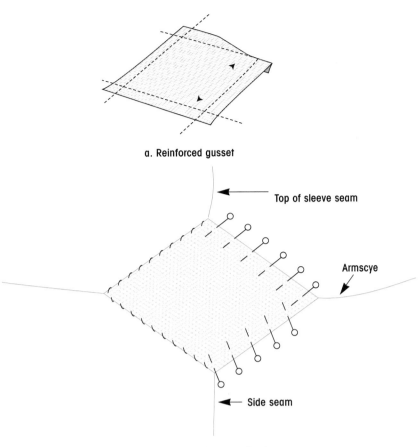

a. Reinforced gusset

b. Gusset being sewn in place

Figure 3-123: This diamond-shaped gusset was reinforced with stitching around its edges (a). The gusset is placed on the bias and fell stitched into place (b).

Insert Hanging Loops, Bra Carriers, and Sleeve Stays

Insert hanging loops, bra carriers, and sleeve stays into sleeves before binding the sleeve.

Hanging loops are essential not only to secure the gown to the hanger, but to help it maintain its shape while hanging. Although the gown shouldn't be hung for long-term storage (it is best wrapped in cotton—an old cotton sheet is ideal), there are times when the gown needs to be on a hanger.

Anchor hanging loops for an off-the-shoulder dress in the stitching line at the bottom of the armscye, or stitch them at either side of each armscye near the top of the seam. This way, the gown will hang from four points instead of the customary two. When not being used to support the gown, the ribbon falls, and follows the curve of the lower

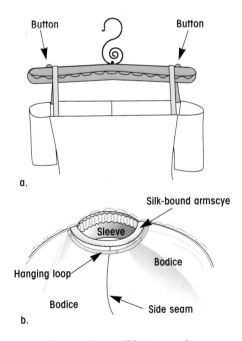

Figure 3-124: Sew small buttons on the top of the hanger to prevent the loops from slipping off, and hang the gown from four anchor points (a). When the gown is worn, the loops fall along the armscye, invisible (b).

part of the armscye, where it rests, out of sight, while the dress is being worn (Figure 3-124).

For gowns with shoulders, loop placement can vary. If the sleeve is full and opaque, then sew hanging loops at the top of the armscye; the shoulders of the gown are on the hanger, and the hanging loops hook around the neck of the hanger (Figure 3-125). When the gown is being worn, the hanging loops tuck out of sight into the fullness of the sleeve. If the sleeve is not opaque or is tight-fitting and cannot risk a ridge from hanging loops, place the loops in the armscye in the manner of an off-the-shoulder gown or anchor them at the underarm. If they are long and fall toward the bodice when the gown is being worn, be sure that they aren't detectable through a tight-fitting bodice.

a.

b.

Figure 3-125: Fasten the hanging loops around the neck of the hanger (a); when the gown is worn, the loops will disappear into the fullness of the sleeve (b).

Unusual solutions sometimes work: I once made a black lace top, which had narrow shoulder seams and full, bell-shaped sleeves, which was to be worn over a strapless gown. The top wasn't underlined, and there was no place to hide hanging loops. My solution was to sew one part of the snap to the inside of the shoulder seam of the top (the black snap was practically invisible and undetectable to the wearer); the other part of the snap was sewn to the hanger. The garment simply snapped in place when it was put on the hanger.

Bra carriers are essential for any gown with shoulders. They do more than simply keep the bra straps out of sight; they anchor the gown to the bra. Make the carriers from a narrow piece of ribbon or a thread chain (Figure 3-126). Bra carriers have other uses as well. A second set can anchor the bra further down the neck edge. They also can be used to secure the gown to its hanger, fastening around a small piece of ribbon that has been sewn to a fabric-covered hanger.

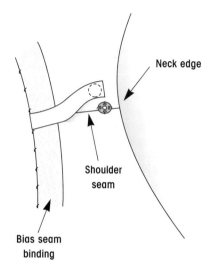

Figure 3-126: *Place bra carriers at the top of the shoulder; the snap mustn't be too close to the neck edge or it will be visible while the gown is being worn.*

Anchor sleeve stays for puffed or leg-of-mutton sleeves at the armscye. The outer sleeve stay attaches at the shoulder and the outer sleeve edge; the inner sleeve stay attaches at the underarm and the inner sleeve edge.

Bind the Seam Allowance

Bind the seam allowance with a bias strip of silk; a scrap from the lining is perfect (Figure 3-127). Silk binding is pleasing to look at and comfortable next to the skin. As tempting as it would be to put the bias binding on by machine, don't do it; accuracy couldn't be assured. The bulkiness of the sleeve and bodice would ensure difficulty—and the bias would be practically guar-

Figure 3-127: *Place a strip of silk bias along the armscye, its folded edge just covering the stitching line. Fell stitch it in place, first along one edge, then the other.*

anteed to slip and result in not-true bias as well as inconsistency of width. Control is far superior by hand. As lightweight lining silk is used for the bias binding, bulk isn't added.

The strip of silk needed for binding an armscye is usually not longer than 12 inches or so for an off-the-shoulder sleeve, and 18 inches or so for a set-in sleeve. Cut an approximately 2-inch-wide strip, then press it lightly down the center. Turn the raw edges in as you stitch the strip in place. Sew one side first (usually the bodice side), then the

other (Figure 3-128). It is hard to get at the second edge of the armscye binding: It's a curved seam, and the area can be further crowded by the presence of elastic. Sometimes turning the sleeve inside out is a help, sometimes not.

After binding the seam allowance of an off-the-shoulder sleeve, tack it to the bodice or sleeves (Figure 3-129). Although the seam allowance often

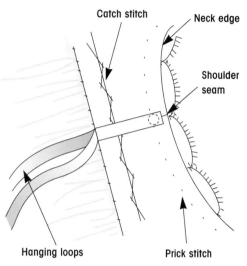

Figure 3-129: *Catch stitch the seam allowance in place at the top of the shoulder; it is usually turned toward the bodice. Placing a row of prick stitches around the neckline, and tack the lining to the inner layers to prevent it from shifting.*

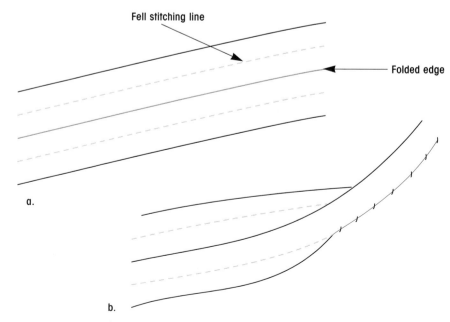

Figure 3-128: *Press the bias strip of silk gently in half lengthwise. Turn the edges under as you fell stitch them in place.*

goes more easily in the direction of the bodice, there are times when it prefers to go the other way. For a fully set-in sleeve, catch stitch the seam allowance in the shoulder area.

JOINING THE BODICE AND THE SKIRT

Although sometimes somewhat unwieldy, joining the bodice and the skirt is a straightforward process, as long as the proper groundwork has been laid. It is the final major construction task, and its successful accomplishment marks the near-completion of the gown. It is an exciting point at which to arrive.

Mark the Seamline

Mark the bottom seamline of the bodice carefully, making certain that matching seamlines are even in length and any angled seams are symmetrical, with both back openings precisely the same length. Although the lining has been sewn around the top and back edges of the bodice, it remains loose at the base of the bodice until after the bodice and skirt have been sewn together.

Finish Preparing the Skirt

In the skirt, gathers should be in place and the gathering threads secured. The seam allowance should be pressed. Continue the gathers as close to the back opening as possible. They will help camouflage the opening, and the area would look strangely flat if ungathered.

Place pleats perfectly, and tack them firmly so they don't shift during stitching; their multiple layers can get very thick, and the weight of the presser foot often causes them to shift during stitching.

The skirt lining may or may not be in place at this point. In the case of gathered and pleated skirts, the lining

Figure 3-130: When preparing piping, a row of basting close to the eventual stitching line will keep the bias from shifting.

is often gathered and pleated along with the fashion fabric. Sometimes, for the sake of reducing bulk, the lining of a gathered skirt is pleated instead of gathered, or it is cut with less fullness. In either of these cases, tack the lining in place by hand (along the seamline) after the waist seam has been sewn and before the bodice lining has been fell stitched in place.

Sometimes, the waist seam is accented with a row of piping, usually self-covered. Cut the piping accurately, otherwise the clean effect it gives will be spoiled by drag lines. Piece the bias carefully, placing any joins as inconspicuously as possible and not on top of bulky seams. Use rattail cord; its thickness is good for piping, and it doesn't have the ridges that cabled cord has. Enclose the cord in a strip of bias, and hand-baste the two edges together (Figure 3-130). The smallest amount of slippage will cause ripples in bias, and basting will help prevent this. Machine stitch it, and apply it to the bodice. Clip the seam allowance of the piping when shaping it around curves, especially at the center V if it is being used with a basque waist.

Measure the Skirt Opening

Carefully measure the skirt opening, which is usually at the center back, to be certain the length is the same on both sides (Figure 3-131). A certain amount of finishing of the opening can be done at this point, before the skirt is sewn to the bodice. Treat the seam allowance at the opening, either by slip stitching it to the lining, hand overcasting the seam allowance, or adding a

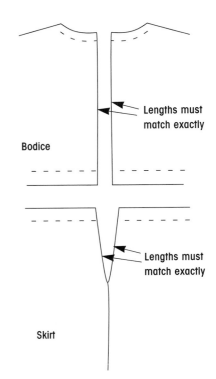

Figure 3-131: Check the lengths of the center back edges of the bodice and skirt. Adjust any discrepancies, even tiny ones, before stitching the bodice–skirt seam.

small placket (an underlap) by hand or machine. Sometimes a hand-picked zipper can be installed at the center back skirt opening; although appropriate in some cases, it is usually not used in a full skirt, as its stiffness would contrast with the soft gathers.

Join the Bodice and Skirt

Once the bodice and skirt are ready, match them carefully and baste them together. (Information on joining basque waists and skirts is found on page 95.) The bodice–skirt seam can be sewn by hand, which guarantees perfect placement and spacing, especially of gathers. (There are times when wrestling an enormous skirt and bodice with full sleeves into the sewing machine is simply too difficult, and accuracy is bound to be compromised.) Stitch with double-thread coated with beeswax, and use a backstitch. Unless the skirt is enormously heavy or has a very long train or has a heavy detachable train, the weight of the skirt is usually well-enough distributed so that there isn't too much strain on a hand-stitched seam.

Whether sewing by hand or machine, don't pull skirt gathers too

tight; otherwise they will pucker the base of the bodice. If there is overhanging lace at the bottom of the bodice, fold it out of the way during stitching. Take care with the placement of gathers; they will affect how the entire skirt will hang.

Finish the Loop Side

The left back center line of the bodice (the line along which the loops are sewn) will line up with the left back edge of the skirt. Once the skirt and bodice have been sewn together, fold the bodice–skirt seam allowances toward the bodice, and fold the bodice center back seam

allowance inward, placing the loops in their final position (Figure 3-132).

Finish the Button Side

There are a number of possibilities for the right back. In the center back of some skirts, the edges abut and there is no placket or underlap on the right side (with certain zippers, for example). In these cases, line the skirt edge up with the center back line of the right back bodice. After stitching the bodice and skirt together, turn the waistline seam allowances toward the bodice (Figure 3-133). (This would leave an opening in the skirt, just below the waist, but as long as it would be covered with a fashion detail such as silk flowers, an underlap or a placket wouldn't be necessary.)

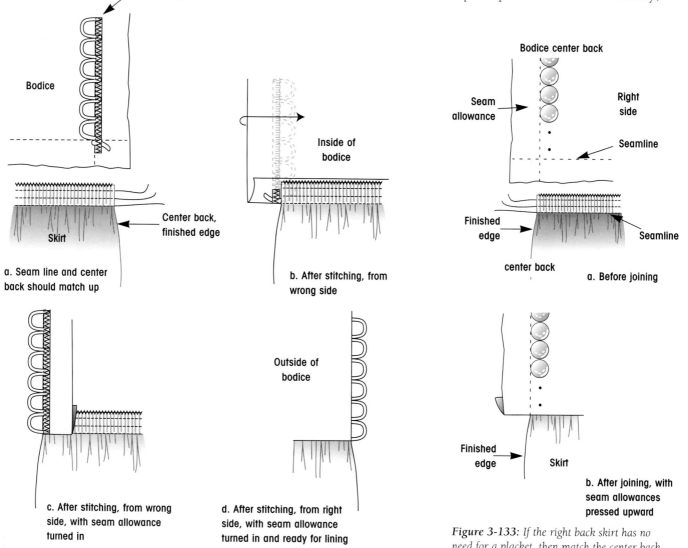

Figure 3-132: The center back of the bodice and the center back of the skirt must match exactly. After stitching the bodice and skirt together, turn the seam allowances inward, and the loops will fold into place. The lining will eventually cover all the seam allowances.

Figure 3-133: If the right back skirt has no need for a placket, then match the center back of the skirt with the center back of the bodice. The bodice back seam allowance will eventually be covered by the lining.

Attaching a Bodice with a Basque Waist

The basque (V) waist is frequently used in wedding gowns, and it is flattering when properly proportioned, sturdily underlined, and well made. The following steps will guarantee its success.

Check the Slope. If there has been an alteration to the slope of the bottom of the bodice (adjusting the V, for example), then make the alteration to the skirt as well; they must have the same slope. The slope in the skirt occurs over a much broader distance, but, once gathered, they are the same (Figure 3-134). The correct slope will be especially noticeable with textured fabrics, such as shantung, douppioni, or faille.

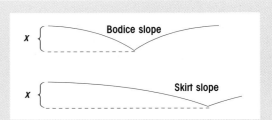

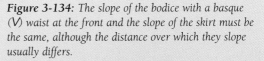

Figure 3-134: The slope of the bodice with a basque (V) waist at the front and the slope of the skirt must be the same, although the distance over which they slope usually differs.

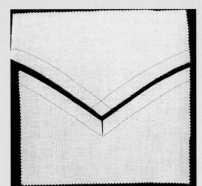

Figure 3-135: Prepare the skirt and bodice for the basque waist with staystitching, decreasing the stitch size toward the center. Clip the seam allowance of the skirt into the V.

Strengthen the Center Front. Reinforce the V at the center front of the skirt with a piece of silk organza, cut with the same grain as the skirt. Staystitch both sides of the V, decreasing the stitch in size toward the center. After stitching, clip the seam allowance vertically to the bottom of the V but not through the staystitching (Figure 3-135).

Staystitch the Bodice. Stitch the waistline with two rows of staystitching (one on either side of the V), crossing them exactly at the center front of the V and extending them into the seam allowances. Check after staystitching that the fashion fabric of the bodice is taut; otherwise a bubble will form at the base of the V, spoiling the effect of the basque waist.

Start to Stitch. The rows of staystitching on the bodice and the skirt not only stabilize the area, but serve as stitching guidelines. With right sides of the fabric together and the bodice on the bottom, pin the right bodice to the right skirt. Begin stitching in the seam allowance of the left bodice, proceed to the V (at which point the skirt is being stitched as well), and continue along the seamline for several inches, following the staystitching. Half of the basque waist is now stitched.

Finish Attaching the Bodice. To finish attaching the bodice to the skirt, pin the left skirt to the left bodice, beginning several inches away from the V. Starting at the side seam, stitch the skirt and the bodice, proceed toward the V, cross the other row of stitches at the center front (at which point the skirt will no longer be stitched on), and continue onto the right seam allowance (Figure 3-136). As you stitch, shift the bulk of the skirt from one side to the other; the clipped seam allowance makes this easy. The stitches should have covered all the staystitches; if not, go over them carefully so that they do (Figure 3-137).

Fold the Seam Allowances. Turn the seam allowances toward the bodice (Figure 3-138). There is some bulk at the V, but the seam allowances can be folded quite flat and held in place with a basting stitch or two. There should be sufficient underlining in the bodice to mask the seam allowances. If necessary, add extra boning at this point for better definition of the basque waist. the boning channels can be hand stitched to the underlining.

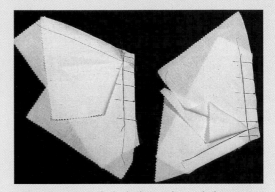

Figure 3-136: With the bodice underneath, begin stitching in the seam allowance. Joining the skirt at the center front, stitch the seam. Reposition the skirt, and stitch the second half of the basque waist: Starting several inches from the center front, stitch the skirt and the bodice together, heading toward the center front. Continue stitching onto the seam allowance of the bodice.

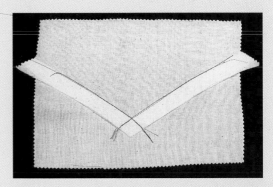

Figure 3-137: When stitched properly, the seamlines duplicate the staystitching lines and form an X which crosses exactly at the center front.

Figure 3-138: Basque waist seam allowances usually turn toward the bodice; sufficient underlining prevents the seam allowances from being detected on the fashion fabric.

Figure 3-139: If the right back skirt extends to form a small underlap—as on this linen skirt—extend it beyond the center line as far as necessary and add small snaps. The bodice back seam allowance is covered by the lining.

If the skirt edge is to form a small underlap, then extend it as necessary beyond the center line. Sew small snaps on the underlap, and sew the matching halves of the snaps to the left side of the skirt. Stitch them to the lining or the seam allowance so that the stitches don't show through to the fashion fabric (Figure 3-139).

If there is a separate placket, then line up the center seamline of the skirt with the center back line of the bodice. Machine or hand stitch the placket. Sew snaps on the placket, and sew their matching halves to the left side of the skirt, stitching them to the lining or the seam allowance (Figure 3-140).

Trim the Bodice–Skirt Seam

Trim the waist seam, but not at the expense of destabilizing it or of creating a short, thick ridge. A heavy gathered skirt will lose its stability if the rows of gathering stitches are cut into. Remove the row of zigzagging on the gathers, however, if it is bulky, and trim the extra fabric above the topmost row of gathers. The bodice seam can be trimmed down a little, and extra lace and ornamentation can be trimmed out of the seam allowance. Neat, well-behaved seam allowances, trimmed free of loose threads and placed carefully where they belong, are more important than overly trimmed seam allowances.

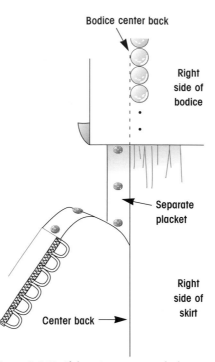

Figure 3-140: If there is a separate placket, then line up the center back lines of the bodice and skirt; the skirt placket and the bodice seam allowance both extend beyond the center line. Turn the bodice–skirt seam allowances toward the bodice. The bodice back seam allowance will eventually be covered by the lining.

Attend to the Finishing Details

ATTACH BUTTONS. Sew the remaining buttons to the base of the bodice, reinforcing the bottom button, as it is often used as the central bustling button, bearing much of the weight of the skirt.

INSERT THE BONING. Add the boning to its channels and secure each piece with a few stitches at the base of the channel. Turn the seam allowances toward the bodice; this will cover the base of the channels, further securing the boning.

ATTACH THE LINING. Stitch the lining along the waistline, carefully positioning it so that there is no bagging or pulling. Fold it at the back opening so that all raw edges are covered (Figure 3-141).

ATTACH FASTENERS. Sew a small snap at the top of the center back to keep the right bodice placket flat against the left bodice. Sew a small hook and eye at the bottom of the center back, at the edge of the right bodice placket and at the matching place at the base of the left bodice to relieve some of the strain on the lowest buttons (Figures 3-142 and 3-143).

ATTACH HANGING LOOPS. Heavy skirts sometimes benefit from their own hanging loops, which can attach at the side of the skirt. The weight, however, will be better distributed if they attach to four points, much like suspenders. They fall out of sight when the gown is being worn (Figure 3-144).

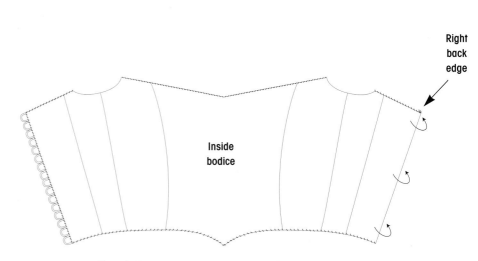

Figure 3-141: Fell stitch the lining around the entire inside of the bodice: around the neck edge, down the side with the loops, along the bottom edge, and along the extended right back edge, where it has wrapped around to the front to cover the right center back seam allowance.

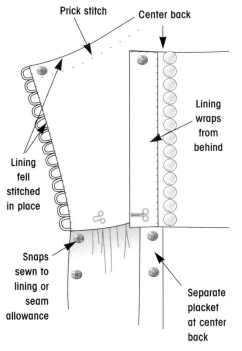

Figure 3-142: *Internal hardware can assure that layers stay put: Snaps and hooks and eyes are small enough to be inconspicuous (if snaps are large, cover them with pieces of silk).*

Figure 3-144: *Hook the skirt's separate hanging loops around the neck of the hanger (a); they fall into the body of the skirt when the gown is being worn (b).*

Figure 3-143: *In this gown, the boning has been put into its channels and secured, hanging loops are in place, and all seam allowances are hidden inside the lining, which has been fell stitched into place. A row of prick stitches along the neck edge keeps the lining from shifting. The waistline stay emerges through the openings in the lining and fastens with hooks and eyes. A hook and eye and snaps keep the underlap in place.*

Add Any Zippers

Although most wedding gowns fasten with loops and fabric-covered (or pearl) buttons, there are instances the hand-picked zipper is used. It's a couture touch that is easy to install, secure from the wearer's point of view, and clean and elegant to look at.

Prepare the opening—which can be at the center back or along the side seam—for a centered zipper application. Add some internal stabilizing to the seam allowances, especially if any of the seams are off grain, and baste seam allowances in place to prevent any shifting of layers. Then, using double thread, which you've coated with beeswax, sew the zipper in place with a prick stitch. Begin stitching at the top of one side of the zipper, working your way down to the bottom. Finish off the thread. With a new piece of thread, begin at the bottom of the other side and work your way up to the top of the zipper. This will allow you to properly align the fabric as you sew, eliminating any puckers or gaps. Add a hook and eye to the top of the zipper placket. Zippers can also be used at the wrist; an adequate length here is about four inches.

Ornamentation and Bustling

Sometimes the entire dress is conceived around the details; sometimes the details are an afterthought. These details—silk flowers or a lush bow with long, sweeping tails—can be the spark that lights the way for the rest of the gown, and sometimes they're the finishing touch, the missing piece of the puzzle, the final brush stroke on the canvas.

ORNAMENTATION

If ever there were a case for gilding the lily, it would be with a wedding gown. Wedding gowns present wonderful opportunities for ornamentation; the whole nature of the gown lends itself to fantasy and embellishment. Flowers, bows, and sashes can all provide wonderful and stylistically important interest to a gown. They add dimension, color, whimsy, contrast, and richness. The addition of a simple cluster of silk flowers, or just the right bow in just the right place can transform a gown from something lovely into something very lovely (Figure 3-145).

Figure 3-145: An antique velvet ribbon adds a soft touch of color to this understated gown.

Flowers add color, dimension, and give a gown a wonderful lift (Figure 3-146). They can be made from the fashion fabric, or from something else. They can have self-fabric leaves, or contrasting leaves, there can be trailing stems with rosebuds at the ends of them (Figures 3-147 and 148). And there can be tendrils of ivy. A flower can combine different fabrics: Two layers of

Figure 3-146: These silk flowers echo the colors that appear in the sequins of the lace bodice at right. Their placement adds dimension and a focal point to the front of the dress.

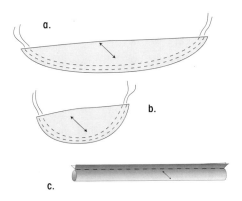

Figure 3-147: Gather, roll, and hand stitch a long, bias strip of fabric to form a rose (a); and place pearl sprays in its center. A number of smaller pieces of fabric can be gathered and overlapped to make a cabbage rose (b), and a long, narrow bias tube with a rose inserted at one end can duplicate a stem (c).

silk georgette, each layer a different color, can be rolled into a luscious rose.

Flowers are often placed at the base of the bodice in the back of a gown, either in a cluster or a crescent, or at the side front. They can accentuate the shoulders of a gown, positioned around an off-the-shoulder sleeve, or they can echo the entire neckline. They can also be used on the skirt—nestled within

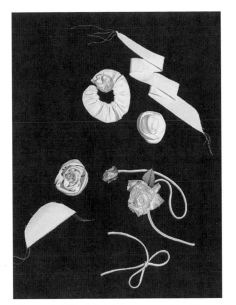

Figure 3-148: Self-fabric roses and trailing stems are easy to make; properly proportioned and well placed, they make a beautiful focal point for a gown.

the ruffles of a gown, or strewn along the back of a train. The possibilities are endless, and it is sometimes their unexpected placement that gives them added charm and impact.

Whether created from self-fabric, contrasting fabric, or self-fabric lined with a contrasting fabric, bows look beautiful on a gown (Figure 3-149). As with the gown itself, proportion is critical, both in width and height. Some

Figure 3-149: Bows are a wonderful chance to add style and charm; choices in size, style, fabrication and placement are endless.

points to ponder: Should the bow be tailored, with carefully placed tucks, absolutely uniform on each side? Or should it be soft and loose, looking as if it were just tied? Should there be tails?

Bows can be soft, or they can be stiffened internally with horsehair or net. They can be combined with flowers, or they can be embellished with lace appliqués. They can appear on the shoulders or at the wrists. A series of small bows can run up the front or back of the gown, or they can be placed along the center back seam and figure into the design of the gown once it is bustled. They also provide wonderful camouflage for the back placket of the skirt as well as the bustling buttons and loops.

BUSTLED TRAINS

When a long wedding gown skirt is bustled, the gown is suddenly transformed. Few dresses ever make such a dramatic transition: Initially worn in a formal, ceremonial setting, the gown is now something in which to celebrate.

Although the formula for bustling is straightforward, bustling a gown can sometimes be a frustrating process, requiring endless adjustments and fine-tuning. Some gowns bustle like magic; others seem to put up a fight, when even the most concerted efforts can lead to less-than-perfect results. There are many variables: the fullness of the skirt, the fullness of the crinoline, and most critical, the slope of the hem as the train lengthens. Achieving a satisfactory result can, at times, be a lengthy process.

There are a few instances in which bustling doesn't work. Fishtail hems give a wonderful effect, but they usually don't bustle very successfully; the wearer has to be careful, realizing that the fishtail is something of a liability, and that effect, rather than ease of wear, is the primary focus. Tulle trains are also difficult to bustle attractively. There can be eight to ten layers of tulle in the skirt (the charm of a tulle skirt lies in its fullness and loft). If bustled in the traditional manner, there can be too much fullness and too much loft. It may be better to cut the layers to ankle length or to a graceful sweep length (a very modest train). If bustling is insisted upon, consider layer by layer bustling; (bustling one layer at a time). Although tedious to do, the effect of controlled fullness may be better than too much fullness.

Traditional Bustling

Long wedding gowns are usually bustled in the traditional manner: The skirt is picked up at the appropriate point(s) and fastened to the back waist. Bustling is usually accomplished by loops on the skirt that fasten to buttons at the base of the bodice.

When first creating the bustle, the gown should be hemmed and the bride should be wearing the appropriate undergarments and shoes. Finding the appropriate points at which to lift the skirt is largely a matter of trial and error, but there are a few guidelines.

FIND A PICKUP POINT. First, find the point on the center back skirt seam from which, once attached to the base of the bodice, the skirt will fall so that its hem just touches the floor. A loop will be sewn to that point on the skirt, and it will fasten around the lowest bodice button. At the moment, simply pin it securely to the base of the bodice.

FIND ADDITIONAL PICKUP POINTS. Next, determine which other parts of the skirt will need to be lifted. Try along the side back seam. Again, find the point that will enable the skirt to skim the floor; attach this pickup point to a point along the waist seam (at which a bustling button will be sewn) an inch or two to one side of the point at which the center back of the skirt is pinned.

LOCATE THE REMAINING POINTS. Continue the procedure, if necessary; there may be a pickup point between the one on the center back seam and the one on the side back seam. The heavier and fuller the skirt, the more pickup points, and the more buttons along the waist seam. There will always be an odd number of buttons: the center pickup point plus pairs of pickup points to either side. Don't extend the pickup points as far as the side seam of

Figure 3-150: Here is the gown before bustling. Carefully and accurately mark the bustling pickup points with pins.

the gown; the hem there is at floor level and needn't be bustled. Further, the front of the dress would be pulled and the silhouette of the gown would be distorted. The pickup points, once released, will form a horseshoe shape on the back of the gown (Figures 3-150 and 3-151). It is sometimes easier to pin one side correctly, and later match the other side, once the dress is on a flat surface. Bustling a gown, especially if

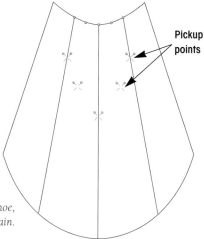

Pickup points

Figure 3-151: The bustling points form a horseshoe, echoing the slope of the hem of the train.

Figure 3-152: This gown has been bustled; the bustling buttons are barely visible at the base of the heavily embellished bodice.

button fits through them, but tight enough that the button can't slip out.

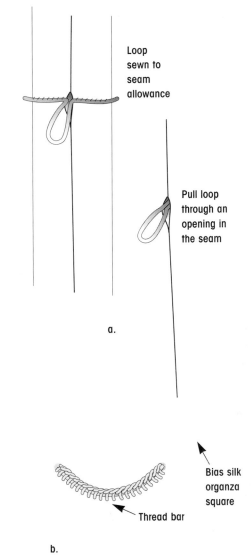

Loop sewn to seam allowance

Pull loop through an opening in the seam

a.

Bias silk organza square

Thread bar

b.

Figure 3-153: Hide small pieces of the soutache looping on the inside of the skirt along the seams, and pull them to the outside from a small hole in the seam when needed (a). Alternatively, make thread bars loops. Reinforce the loops on the underside with a small bias square of silk organza (b).

the train is long and heavy, can be a lengthy process.

ATTACH THE BUTTONS. Sew the bustling buttons, apart from the lowest center back button (which functions as part of the gown's closure and is already in place), along the base of the bodice, to either side of the center (Figure 3-152). There is often a stylistic detail there which can hide them: overhanging lace, flowers, a bow, or a peplum. Even if the buttons are not hidden, the

veil often camouflages them, and in any event, they are barely noticeable.

ATTACH THE LOOPS. Bustling loops can hide in the seams (if that is where they are placed), or they can appear on the surface of the skirt. Reinforce the loop area (on the inside of the skirt) with a square of silk organza or fashion fabric. If they are in-seam, form the loops from a piece of soutache braid, or create a loop from a thread bar (Figure 3-153). Make the loops loose enough that the

Attaching a Bustle with Ribbons

There are times when the skirt is more beautiful if it is bustled another way: Rather than lifting the pickup points to the top of the skirt, they are tucked under the skirt (Figure 3-154). The principle of pickup points on the

Figure 3-154: The effect of the tiers on this skirt would be lost if it were bustled in the conventional manner.

skirt) will join the matching ribbons at the waist and tie (Figure 3-157). Match the colors of each skirt ribbon to its appropriate bodice ribbon. Pairs of colors will be much easier to match up than a sea of white ribbons. The effect on the outside is of an overhang (Figure 3-158).

Figure 3-156: Place ribbons in a horseshoe formation on the inside of the skirt, and line them up with the waistline ribbons. Stitch them in place.

skirt with match points along the waistline is the same, but instead of loops and buttons, pairs of ribbons are used. Rather than being joined on the outside of the gown, they are joined on the inside. It is worth experimenting to see which way of bustling is more beautiful.

ATTACH RIBBONS TO THE BODICE.
Sew a series of ribbons to the inside of the base of the bodice; one at the center, and others to either side of the center, exactly in the manner of the outside bustling buttons.

ATTACH RIBBONS TO THE SKIRT.
Sew ribbons at the pickup points on the inside of the skirt (Figure 3-155 and 3-156). These ribbons (which should be color-coordinated and light in color so that they are not visible through the

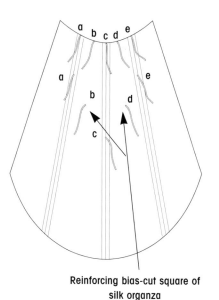

Reinforcing bias-cut square of silk organza

Figure 3-155: Ribbon placement mimics that of the bustling loops, but the ribbons are on the inside of the gown, not the outside. Pairs of pastel ribbons will be easy to match up.

Figure 3-157: Tie the ribbons securely; double knots are a good idea, especially with slippery satin ribbon.

Figure 3-158: The effect of the tiers is preserved and the doubled fabric adds extra fullness to the back of the skirt, enhancing the appeal of the ruffles.

DETACHABLE TRAINS

Trains can, of course, be detachable, in which case the nature of the dress changes dramatically. Also, there are instances when a train is so lengthy and heavy that bustling it would be difficult in terms of both comfort and engineering.

Construct the Train

The fullness at the top of the train needs to be controlled: The train can be gathered along its top edge, but pleats will give a flatter look while maintaining the width of the train. Detachable trains usually need to be pieced (use two side seams; they're less conspicuous than a center back seam). Piping

around the outer edge of the train will give it definition and stability.

The gown must be engineered from within to bear the weight of a heavy train. Use the inside waistline stay to help you anchor the weight of the detachable train, which should hang from the waist rather than from the shoulders or neck of the gown.

Line the Train

The train must glide. If the fabric in any way pulls or hesitates, line it (consider the surface along which it will be pulled; most gown fabrics glide easily, but there are exceptions).

Although unwieldy, trains are easy to line. Cut the lining and the fashion fabric exactly the same, stitch right sides together, trim and clip around curves, and turn the train right side out. Once the lining is in place, the top edges of the train and lining must be realigned,

making sure that the lining isn't visible when the train is spread out

Attach the Train

Hooks and eyes usually attach detachable trains to the gown; buttons would be cumbersome and snaps would never hold the weight of the train (Figure 3-159). Sew the hooks on the train and the eyes on the gown; after the train is removed, the eyes are not only less conspicuous than the hooks, but they are also unlikely to catch on anything, especially lace. Space the hooks and eyes closely together; the more points the train hangs from the better—its weight will be distributed and there will be fewer and shorter gaps between the points at which it attaches. Camouflage the attachment area with a peplum, bow, flowers, or a sash, if necessary.

Figure 3-159: This detachable train is secured with frequently placed hooks and eyes. They are hidden from sight by the skirt's built-in, overhanging bustle.

4

APPLICATION

The Making of Four Gowns

"Fashion is a craft, a poetic craft."

—Yves St. Laurent

A Romantic Pink Gown

This guipure lace gown whispers its pink undertones: a pink underbodice, discreet stripes on an ivory organza overskirt revealing a pink underskirt, and pink roses at the back waist.

Proportion is critical with this softly romantic gown. With its subtle play between pink and cream, gentle touches abound: the overhang of the lace at the bottom of the sleeves that echoes the overhang of the lace at the bottom of the bodice, the careful matching of the stripes on the skirt, the band of guipure lace roses that appears to continue around the top of the gown, the carefully made buttons that are layered, as is the skirt, with silk organza over pink taffeta.

CONSTRUCTION OF THE PINK GOWN

Fabrication

Guipure lace and pink satin are the main fabrics in the bodice. I found a pink satin with a lovely sheen and of a good weight. (Heavy satin and guipure lace, along with underlining and lining, would have been too thick, but I didn't want anything too flimsy, either.) While Alençon lace has a net background which obscures the finish of the underlying fabric, guipure, like eyelet, has holes in it that allow the texture of the background fabric to show through.

An off-white striped silk organza was used for the overskirt. The original stark white of the guipure lace contrasted too sharply with the off-white organza, but careful dyeing of the lace with tea created just the right color. After pressing the organza, I examined it to determine if there was a difference in the two sides. The satin stripes seemed matte on one side and shiny on the other, and although either would have been fine, I chose the matte-finished side.

The pink taffeta I chose for the underskirt was lighter in weight but the same color as the pink satin of the bodice. The taffeta and the organza work well together in the skirt in terms of loft and weight. A separate purchased crinoline will be worn with the gown.

Silk flowers were later found at Dulken and Derrick in New York (see Resources) and placed at the base of the bodice (and perhaps at the center back or sides of the dress).

The Muslin

The muslin for this gown was straightforward: close-fitting, off-the-shoulder, with short sleeves and a dropped waist (Figure 4-1). I adapted the design from a Butterick wedding gown pattern, changing the neckline from a shallow V to a gentle scoop and the waistline from a basque waist to a straight, dropped waist. The well-boned bodice received additional support from the waistline stay.

I could not determine the final sleeve length until I finalized the placement of the lace motifs on the sleeve. Using the muslin, I made some engineering decisions about the sleeves. Elastic in a casing independent of the sleeve would provide more freedom of movement than a form-fitting sleeve would. I also planned to stiffen the actual sleeves, which would allow them to stand slightly away from the shoulders.

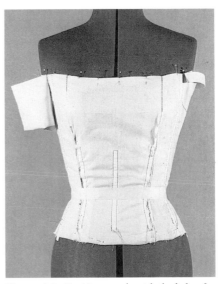

Figure 4-1: *Decisions made with the help of the muslin included placement of the sleeves, waistline stay, and boning.*

The Bodice

I chose muslin as an underlining for the bodice. After sewing preshrunk boning channels to the underlining, I basted together the underlining and satin. Next, I stitched the front and back princess seams; trimmed, clipped, and pressed them; and catch stitched them in place. The side seams could not be stitched until after the lace was applied. The seamlines at the top of the bodice pieces were staystitched, turned in, then catch stitched in place. Twill tape wasn't necessary along these seamlines; they weren't cut on the bias, and the addition of twill tape would have removed the natural movement of this fabric, making the gown very restricting to wear. The back openings, center front, and seamline at the bottom of the bodice were all carefully marked with contrasting thread so that they would be visible when working on the lace.

The Sleeves

The sleeve muslin was placed underneath the guipure lace. Although the sleeve length was roughly known, its exact length depended on where the motifs fell (Figure 4-2). The placement of the lace on each sleeve was identical. The upper border on the lace was placed so that there was a pretty row of roses along the top of each sleeve.

I layered the sleeves from top to bottom as follows: guipure lace, satin, cotton underlining, and spun silk lining (Figure 4-3). A double layer of one-inch-wide horsehair placed along the top edge of each sleeve stiffened the edge and allowed the sleeve to stand firmly in place, away from the body of the dress. The result was a beautiful, uncrushable curve at the top of the sleeve. The sleeves were lined at this point. I fell stitched the lining at the top and bottom edges of the sleeve and then basted it to the sleeve along the armscye. This row of basting stitches later served as a stitching guide once the sleeves were ready to attach to the bodice.

Placing the Lace on the Bodice

I used one large piece of guipure for the front of the bodice and two smaller pieces for each of the back panels. The guipure lace was densely configured and its horizontal rows of motifs figured importantly in its layout. (Unlike Alençon lace, whose motifs can sometimes appear to be almost random, guipure has extremely visible internal

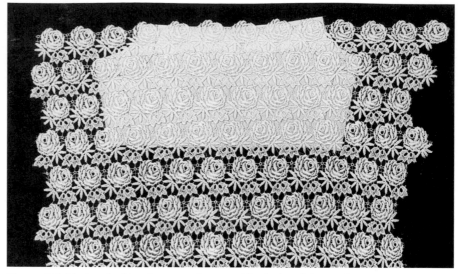

Figure 4-2: The length of the sleeve was determined by the lay of the motifs.

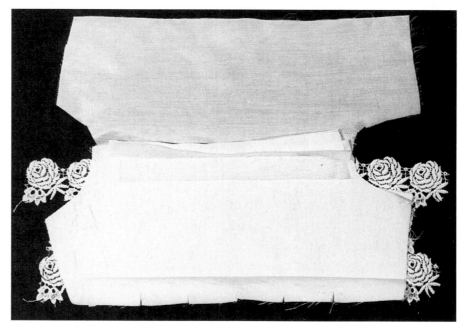

Figure 4-3: The fabric layers, as seen from inside the sleeves, are: guipure lace, satin, cotton underlining, and the spun silk lining.

patterns that must be lined up properly.)

I placed the motifs at the base of the bodice to echo the motifs at the base of the sleeves. From there, the lace extended upward to the top edge of the bodice. Roses along the top of the bodice had to match the roses along the top of the sleeves. The seamline at the base of the bodice was dropped slightly to accommodate the correct position of the top row of roses (Figure 4-4).

Once the lace was correctly placed on the front piece, the lace placement on the back pieces had to match it not only along the bottom edges but also at the side seams (Figure 4-5). On the front bodice piece, the lace was shaped around the bust, and the topmost row of roses at the center was cut away from the rest of the lace and dropped slightly to accommodate the scooped neckline. The roses were then stitched back into place. Similarly, a row of roses at the top edge of the back bodice pieces was cut into a strip and superimposed for correct placement (Figure 4-6).

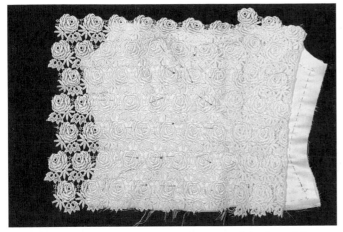

Figure 4-4: *One large piece of guipure lace covered the front of the bodice.*

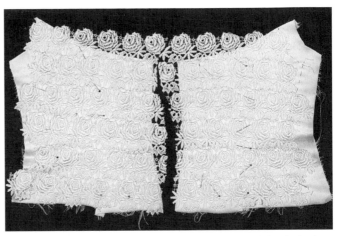

Figure 4-5: *Two smaller pieces of guipure lace were used for the back bodice panels.*

Figure 4-6: *To achieve the same placement as the roses at the top of the sleeves, this row of roses had to be cut into a strip and superimposed on the bodice.*

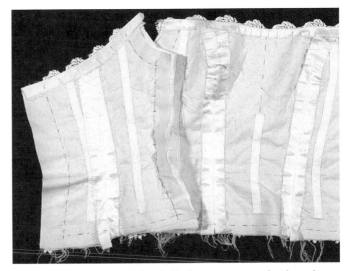

Figure 4-7: *Lace was tacked to the bodice at every motif with stitches that stopped approximately one inch from the side seams and from the seamline at the base of the bodice.*

With placement finalized, I tacked the lace to the bodice at every motif, stopping the tacking stitches approximately one inch from the side seams and one inch from the seamline at the base of the bodice (Figure 4-7). Next, I basted and stitched the side seams of the bodice together, carefully keeping the lace out of the seams. After treating the seam allowances, the lace was overlapped and stitched into place (Figure 4-8).

Loops and Buttons

Once the lace was in place, the loops and buttons were attached (Figure 4-9). The loops and buttons were applied in the standard manner described in

Figure 4-8: *After stitching the side seams and treating the seam allowances, the lace was overlapped and stitched into place.*

Figure 4-9: *Loops were applied to the bodice in the standard manner (left side of bodice back shown).*

"Sleeve Closures" (see page 74). The bottom two or three buttons were left off until the skirt was attached.

Further Work on the Bodice

Next, I tacked the waistline stay into place and prepared the bodice lining. After cutting and marking the lining with white tracing paper, I assembled it. The top edges were staystitched and turned in. The lining was stitched with a fell stitch along the top edges of the bodice and basted in place at the armscye (the basting served as a stitching guide when the sleeves were sewn on). In addition, two buttonholes were made for the waistline stay to exit once the lining was sewn in place (Figure 4-10).

Figure 4-10: *Here, the lining, which has been stitched with a fell stitch along the top edges of the bodice and basted in place at the armscye, is folded back to reveal the waistline stay. Two buttonholes were made so that the waistline stay could exit once the lining was sewn in place.*

I also staystitched the bottom seamline of the lining; this row of stitching later served as a guide for placement when the bottom edge of the lining was stitched in place. A final row of hand stitching was added along the top edge of the bodice: a neat row of small prick stitches about $1/2$ inch below the top

edge, through all layers (except the outermost, and avoiding the boning channels), to ensure that the bodice lining wouldn't shift.

Joining the Sleeves and Bodice

After carefully lining up and matching the roses along the top edge of the

sleeve to the roses along the top edge of the bodice, I stitched the sleeves into the armscye (Figure 4-11). The elastic, in a silk casing, was then stitched in place. The seam allowance was trimmed and bulk (thick little pieces of lace, for example) removed wherever possible. A bias strip of the lining silk was used to bind the seam allowance (Figure 4-12).

Figure 4-11: *After carefully lining up and matching the roses along the top edge of the sleeve to the roses along the top edge of the bodice, I stitched the sleeves into the armscye.*

Figure 4-12: *After joining the bodice and sleeve, elastic—in a silk casing—was stitched into the armscye. Then the seam allowances were bound.*

The Skirts

THE OVERSKIRT

The overskirt was made from silk organza, which had crosswise stripes. If they had run lengthwise, the skirt could have been created from one long gathered piece of material, with a single back seam. Since they didn't, four pieces of material had to be cut, then joined together. Obviously, a center front seam was undesirable, so the seams were shifted to form two side front seams and two side back seams. French seams were used to join the panels (Figure 4-13). The most inconspicuous hem choice was to fold up the organza (in the middle of an organza stripe so that the stripes would line up) and slip stitch it into place (Figure 4-14).

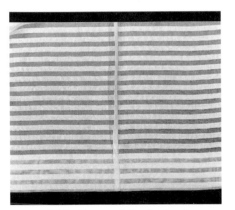

Figure 4-13: After carefully aligning the stripes on two overskirt panels, I used a French seam to join them.

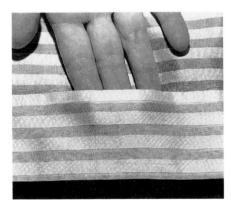

Figure 4-14: For an inconspicuous hem, the organza was folded up (in the middle of a stripe so the stripes could be lined up) and slip stitched into place.

THE UNDERSKIRT

I used taffeta for the underskirt. To avoid the problem of puckering seams (common with tightly woven taffeta), I cut the side seams of the underskirt, which were positioned to match those of the overskirt, slightly off grain. The top circumference was the same as the overskirt's (the two were treated as one), and the tiny difference in hem circumferences was undetectable. To guarantee an even skirt length, the taffeta skirt's hem was curved; it was shaped, edged with hem lace, and stitched into place (Figure 4-15).

Figure 4-15: To ensure even length, the taffeta underskirt's hem was shaped. It was then edged with hem lace and stitched into place.

JOINING THE SKIRTS

Because of the position of the skirt seam, there was no center back opening. One was made by cutting vertically down the center back of each layer. The opening was partially sewn shut from the bottom, in the manner of a dart. The raw edges of the organza folded to the inside (toward the body) and the raw edges of the taffeta folded to the outside (away from the body). The opening on each skirt was layered and its folded edges slip stitched together (Figure 4-16). The skirts were then basted together along the top edge and, thereafter, treated as one.

Just before the skirts were gathered, the center front and sides of the skirts were marked (the skirt seams were neither on the centers nor on the sides of the skirt and couldn't serve as placement guides when joining the skirt to the bodice). The skirts were gathered together, and their gathered seam allowances were pressed (Figure 4-17).

Figure 4-16: To form an opening in the skirt, I made a vertical cut in the center back of the skirt. On the outer layer, the edges of the slit were turned in. On the taffeta, the edges were turned toward the outside. The folded edges were then aligned and slip stitched together.

Figure 4-17: The over- and underskirts were gathered as one. The seam allowance was then pressed to reduce bulk.

Joining the Bodice and Skirts

When the bodice and skirts were ready for joining, I matched the side seams of the bodice to the sides of the skirts, the center front of the bodice to the center front of the skirts, and the

Figure 4-18: *The right edge of the bodice and skirt extend to the left of the center back line, creating an underlap.*

center backs to either side of the back opening. The left skirt opening edge was lined up with the center back of the left bodice (the stitching line for the loops). The right skirt opening edge, rather than lining up exactly with the center back of the bodice, extended very slightly into the seam allowance (Figure 4-18), forming an underlap. The right back bodice extended as well, to form its own underlap for buttoning. The seam was basted, then machine stitched. The waist seam allowances

were folded toward the bodice, and the left center back seam allowance of the bodice was folded in. The layers at the bottom corner of the bodice were tacked to keep them in place, and the remaining buttons were sewn on.

The Lining

Next, the lining was completed. I inserted the bones in their channels and stitched the channels closed. At the left back, the lining was folded along the center back seamline and then fell stitched in place next to the loops. At the right back, the lining was extended past the bodice seam allowance and wrapped around toward the front; the edge was turned under and fell stitched in place. The lining was next sewn across the bottom of the bodice, camouflaging all seam allowances and inner workings.

Hanging Loops

A final touch was the placement of the hanging loops (Figure 4-19), which were made from blue (remember, something blue…) ribbons (they will be invisible from the outside of the dress). I attached the loops to the bodice front and back near the top of the armscye, allowing the dress to hang from four points instead of the customary two. Although not a heavy gown, it benefitted from this more even treatment when hanging. A small hook

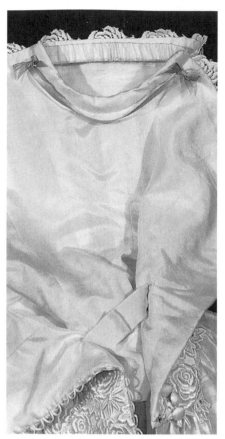

Figure 4-19: *Ribbon hanging loops were attached to the front and back of the bodice near the top of the armscye.*

sewn at the base of the bodice placket and a small snap sewn at the top of the bodice placket held the placket in place. Finally, the flowers were positioned and sewn on.

A Traditional White Gown

This traditional gown, with its full skirt and generously proportioned sleeves, showcases beautiful pearled and sequinned Alençon lace and lustrous silk shantung. Its bodice seams taper to a basque waist (emphasized by the placement of the lace), its pearl buttons down the back of the bodice and on the sleeves echo the pearl clusters on the upper sleeves, and its tiers of lace-edged ruffles cascade down the back panels of the skirt. Clusters of white roses are placed at the base of each upper sleeve and at the center back.

CONSTRUCTION OF THE WHITE GOWN

Fabrication

In addition to the white silk shantung used for this gown, three different Alençon laces were chosen: a wide panel of pearled and sequinned lace, to be used for the bodice appliqués and base of the sleeves; a pearled and sequinned galloon, to be separated and used at the base of the skirt up to the ruffled panels at the back; and finally, an unembellished galloon, to be separated and used to trim the silk organza ruffles.

The Muslin

The muslin for this type of gown, with its extra bodice seams, requires careful fitting (Figure 4-20). I adapted the bodice from a Butterick dress pattern, adding a center front bodice seam, changing the neckline at both the front and back from a scoop to a V, and adding a basque waist. The sleeves were taken from a Vogue bridal pattern, and a standard seven-piece bridal gown skirt was used and shaped along the top edge to mimic the bottom edge of the bodice.

The focus of most gowns is the bodice, and the most prominent part is the center front panel, which here features lace appliqués. Long pieces of boning were placed along the seams of

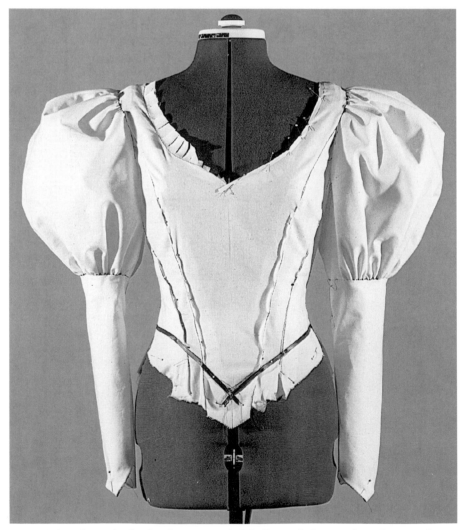

Figure 4-20: *The muslin for the white gown included off-grain bodice seamlines, dramatic sleeves, and a sweetheart neckline.*

the bodice because the seams were, with the exception of the center front and side seams, off grain. They needed to be stretched taut and fortified with boning so that not even the slightest hint of sagging occurred in the bodice. I used twill tape to firm up and stabilize the neckline, which had also been cut off grain, as are most necklines.

The Sleeves

THE UPPER SLEEVES

In this gown, the upper sleeve used a large amount of material (Figure 4-21). If it had been made of lace, not only would it have been costly, but, if embellished, the lace would have been heavy and required considerable inner support (which could have been easily accomplished).

Instead, I embellished the shantung with small clusters of pearls to create surface interest and link the gown's two fabrications with a common element: the pearls. From a technical point of view, the pearls helped strengthen the sleeves: They anchored the fashion fabric to one of the inner layers of net. Such a large expanse of fabric needed support throughout, not just in the sleeve-head area. The fabrics worked together to maintain the loft of the sleeve. Another layer of net and the spun silk lining formed the final two inner layers of the upper sleeve.

THE LOWER SLEEVES

The lower sleeves were made with Alençon lace backed with silk organza. I used two mirror-image lace borders for the sleeves, matching them carefully. After preparing the organza base with staystitching, I basted the lace to it. Then I joined the top and bottom parts of the sleeve and sewed the underarm seam. Next, I sewed the loops and buttons in place (Figure 4-22). On the lower half of the sleeve, I folded over one wide silk organza seam allowance to bind the other seam allowances. On the upper half of the sleeve, I folded over one wide spun silk seam allowance to bind the other seam allowances (Figure 4-23).

INNER SLEEVE SUPPORT

Each sleeve was finished with a piece of elastic (encased in the seam allowance of the horizontal seam that joined the upper and lower seams) and two ribbon stays. The elastic and stays keep the sleeve in place, maintaining its loft and keeping it from sliding down the arm.

Figure 4-22: The lower part of this sleeve was made with Alençon lace and backed with silk organza. It closes with carefully placed loops and pearl buttons.

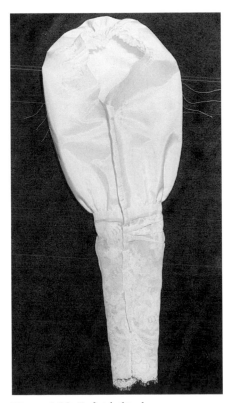

Figure 4-23: To finish this sleeve seam, a wide seam allowance was wrapped around the other seam allowances in both the upper and lower sleeve.

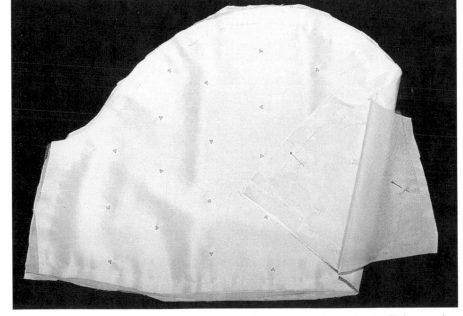

Figure 4-21: The upper sleeves on this gown used a large amount of material. Small clusters of pearls created surface interest and helped join the fashion fabric with an inner layer of net.

The Bodice

BODICE CONSTRUCTION

Two layers of underlining (sheer but crisp cotton batiste and poly-cotton batiste) support the lightweight shantung. The bodice was constructed in the regular manner. The neckline was staystitched, clipped, pressed, and catch stitched in place. Boning is not required to hold the gown up (the shoulders do that); instead, boning serves here to straighten the bodice seams and strengthen the basque waist. It also smooths out the bodice at the side seams and along the back. Rather than being applied in the traditional vertical manner, boning followed the off-grain front bodice seams and was applied after the seams were stitched. Narrow silk organza channels for the boning were held in place with a fell stitch. Not only did this put the boning exactly where it was needed, but the layers (there are six: three layers from the bodice and three layers from the seam allowance) padded and camouflaged the boning's presence (Figure 4-24).

BODICE LACE

Lace appliqués were used to decorate the center front and back panels (Figures 4-25 and 4-26). The seams that shape the bodice provided a good focus for the appliqués. The entire bodice could have been covered with lace, but such a treatment would have obscured the vertical lines that add so much interest to the bodice. A border of the lace was applied to echo the shape of the neckline, and the back panels were designed to mirror one another.

BODICE FINISHING

I sewed loops down the center back seamline of the left back bodice; the left back center seam allowance was turned so that the loops faced toward the center back. Then I lined up the bodice backs and sewed the buttons in place with beeswax-coated thread. (The lowest three buttons were left to be sewn later.) The right back seam allowance was evenly trimmed, but left wide.

Cut from the adjusted muslin, the lining was staystitched around its neck-

Figure 4-24: In this gown, boning was placed to follow the off-grain front bodice seams. The narrow boning channels were made with silk organza and stitched in place with fell stitches. Notice that the multiple layers at the seam allowances pad and camouflage the boning.

Figure 4-25: Notice how the vertical seams in this bodice help draw your attention to the lace-covered panel at the center front.

Figure 4-26: The lace on this bodice back was placed to follow the shape of the neckline and mirror itself on each of the back panels.

line to prevent stretching. The seam allowances were clipped and turned in, and the lining was stitched to the bodice with fell stitches to hold it in place along the top edges (basting stitches hold it in place at the armscye). A row of prick stitches was placed

along the neckline to keep the lining from shifting. I fell stitched the left back lining in place along the row of loops and then wrapped the right back lining around the right seam allowance, which finished off the raw edge and formed an underlay for the loops.

The Skirt

SKIRT CONSTRUCTION

I enhanced the shantung with a silk organza underlining. The underlining added loft, filled out the gathers, reduced wrinkling, and provided a firm base for the hemline lace that I added later. Cut identically, the shantung and the silk organza were basted together and were treated, thereafter, as one. The panels were stitched from the bottom to the top; then their seam allowances were trimmed and finished with a small zigzag stitch.

SKIRT BACK PANELS

Tiers of silk organza ruffles were placed on the two center back panels. After being stitched together, the two back panels were marked with placement lines for the ruffles. When planning the ruffles, I considered the following: the number of tiers, the fullness of the ruffles, the depth (would it be constant or graduate?), and the amount of overhang. I experimented with the fullness; in this case, 250 inches of ruffles were needed (this was the measurement of the ruffles after gathering). If the gathering ratio were two to one, then 500 inches of lace-trimmed organza would be needed; if the ratio were

Figure 4-28: *Each ruffle was sewn in place upside down (as shown in the top ruffle) and then flipped over to hide its seam allowance (as shown in the bottom ruffle).*

three to one, resulting in fuller ruffles, then 750 inches would be needed. In this case, nine yards of a galloon were purchased. After the galloon was cut apart and sewn to the organza base, there were 18 yards, or 648 inches of lace-trimmed organza. The proportion was somewhere between two to one and three to one. The planned overhang was minimal (just enough to cover the placement line of the ruffle below). The motifs on the ruffles were positioned to line up identically at the edges of each ruffle (Figure 4-27). The ruffles were sewn on upside down, so that when they were turned down into place, they hid their own seam allowances (Figures 4-28 and 4-29). After an opening was made in the center of the top ruffle, it was sewn to the on the back skirt panel along with the other ruffles.

Figure 4-27: *Identical motifs are placed at the edges of each ruffle.*

Figure 4-29: *These tiers of ruffles are in place; they have been flipped over to hide their seam allowances.*

Figure 4-30: *The galloon on this skirt was cut apart and applied symmetrically from the center front.*

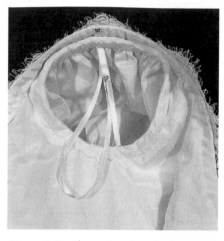

Figure 4-32: *Sleeve stays, hanging loops, and bra carriers were sewn to the seamline of this sleeve. Then a spun silk binding was applied to enclose the raw edges of all the ribbons as well as the seam allowances. The finished seam allowance was tacked toward the neck edge in the vicinity of the shoulder.*

FINISHING THE SKIRT

The skirt was narrowly hemmed by machine, with ½ inch seam lace covering the turned-up raw edge. (As the entire bottom edge was later trimmed with Alençon lace, the stitching would not show). The beaded lace galloon was pressed, cut apart, trimmed, and pieced into one long piece of lace. The galloon was applied symmetrically from the center front of the skirt (Figure 4-30).

Although the lace on the skirt and the lace on the ruffles were not identical, they were similar enough to match up well at the seam that joins the ruffled

panels to the rest of the skirt (Figure 4-31). The many layers in this side seam (the shantung and the underlining of the regular skirt, the shantung, the underlining, the ruffles, and the lace of the back panel), required a spun silk binding on the seam allowance, instead of zigzagging, which would have made the seam allowance stiff. Instead of pressing this seam open, I left it as is, to encourage a soft "rolled" look.

Sleeves

Using a backstitch and beeswax-coated thread, I sewed the sleeves in by hand. The seam allowances were trimmed, but before they were encased in bias strips of spun silk, a few details were added: Sleeve stays were sewn in place along the seamline, as were hanging loops and bra carriers. The binding was then applied to enclose the raw edges of all these ribbons as well as the seam allowances (Figure 4-32). The encased seam allowance was tacked toward the neck edge.

Joining the Skirt and Bodice

After the skirt and bodice were constructed, they were stitched together. Both the bodice and the skirt were staystitched at the center front. In addition, the skirt was prepared for gather-

ing with three rows of gathering stitches on either side of the front V. The basque waist was sewn, first one side, then the other (Figure 4-33), and then the rest of the waist seam was sewn, first one side, then the other (Figure 4-34). Seam allowances were trimmed and pressed toward the bodice. The boning was inserted into its channels, and the lining was fell stitched in place along the waist seam. Pairs of silk roses were stitched in place to decorate each sleeve, and a cluster of roses was attached to the base of the bodice and to the back of the gown.

Bustling

The final touch was the bustling of the gown. Although not overly long, the skirt was full. It would look wonderful when bustled—frothy and feminine. Rather than bustling it in the traditional manner and distorting the ruffles, I chose an Austrian bustle. Lengths of ribbon attached to the inside of the gown at the waistline coordinate with ribbons attached to the skirt at the bustle pickup points. At the appropriate time, the ribbons are tied together. Maintaining its tiered effect, the skirt quickly and easily becomes one length.

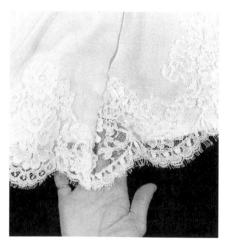

Figure 4-31: *The lace on this skirt and the lace on the ruffles were not identical, but they were similar enough to match up well at the seam that joins the ruffled panels to the rest of the skirt.*

Figure 4-33: As this gown neared completion, the basque waistline seam was sewn (first on one side, then the other), the seam allowances were trimmed, and the waistline seam allowance was pressed upward.

Figure 4-34: There is a small opening in the center of the top ruffle that will be camouflaged by the silk roses.

A Regal Medieval Gown

I call this the medieval gown—closely fitted, with heavy ornamented panels, a square neckline, and fishtail hem. The pleated inserts on the sleeves and at the lower side back seams are reminiscent of the designer Fortuny. Although not a true historic costume, this gown evokes a strong period feeling. Its design, proportions and fabrications all serve the look. With its columnar shape, square neckline, metallic touches, pearls, and long, straight panels, it is not a dress of gentle, soft lines and curves. It must be slim without being tight, regal without being foreboding. An interlocking set of design elements (some of which are somewhat hidden) need to combine and point toward a unified, albeit highly ornamented, whole.

CONSTRUCTION OF THE MEDIEVAL GOWN

Fabrication

Beautifully embellished douppioni was the starting point for this gown. An entire gown of it, combined with other ornamentation, would have been overpowering (not to mention terribly heavy), but well-placed panels of it, long and straight, would put the fabric to good use. The unembellished side panels of the gown needed texture of their own, if not ornamentation, so I matched the color of the embellished douppioni to a plain douppioni. The pleated metallic silk organza somehow seemed medieval to me, and I choose it in a golden color. I also needed a few small pieces of something elegant for underlays (under the base of the pleated organza at the wrists and under the laced panels at the upper back); I found just enough of a golden silk brocade. Finally, as the douppioni was embroidered with pearls (as well as tiny beads and silver bugle beads), I wanted to repeat the pearls somewhere in the gown. I decided to incorporate them into the sleeves and to trim the vertical edges of the neckline with them.

The Muslin

The muslin for this gown was straightforward. I adapted the design from two Vogue dress patterns: one was a knee-length, princess-seamed dress, the neckline of which was square, and the other, a long dress with princess seams, had a fishtail hem (Figure 4-35). There was no boning, nor was there any complicated inner support. I worked out the proportions of the fishtail in the muslin, bearing in mind that the center front and center back panels would be cut from weighty, heavily embellished silk douppioni. Such heavy fabric works best when allowed to hang, and the long, straight panels at the front and back would allow it to do just that.

I had seen a gown with a laced-up back in an Italian bridal magazine and fell in love with it. I was anxious to use the idea but felt it would lie flatter and look better if the lacing were ornamental rather than functional (Figure 4-36). (I decided to have the gown open with a side zipper.) I played with the proportions in muslin: the depth of the panel, whether to use loops or buttonholes. The Italian gown had buttonholes and I liked the look. I experimented with the width of the buttonhole panels and the number and spac-

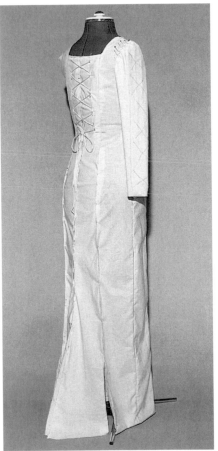

Figure 4-35: The muslin for the Medieval gown provided an opportunity to determine the proportions of the center panels, the fishtail hem, the lacing on the back, and the trimming on the sleeves.

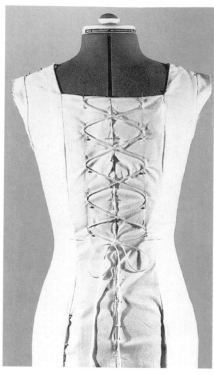

Figure 4-36: Here are the initial plans for the ornamental laced-up panel at the upper back of this gown.

on the sleeve. I decided to hem each layer of the metallic organza before placing it on the muslin (I wanted the bottom edge to ruffle out slightly at the wrist edge, not turn under with the other layers). I realized that once the sleeves were hemmed, the underlying muslin would be visible under the pleated panel at the wrist edge. Therefore, I added a strip of golden silk brocade under the pleated panel; it wasn't necessary to go more than 4 inches or so up from the wrist. Two side panels of douppioni, their raw edges turned in, were stitched to either side of the pleated panel (Figure 4-37). The douppioni and muslin layers were hemmed at the wrist, the seam was stitched, and an opening was left for a four inch zipper. The seam was pressed open, and the zipper was stitched in by hand with a prick stitch. Rows of pearls were created to span the pleated panels. Finally, a lining was cut and inserted. I used fell stitches to hold the lining in place around the bottom edge of the sleeves and around the zippers, and basted it to the seamline at the tops of the sleeves (Figure 4-38).

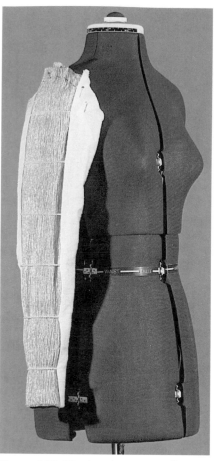

Figure 4-38: The sleeve's center metallic panel was decorated with horizontal rows of pearls.

ing of the buttonholes. For the backing panel, I decided to use a scrap of Chinese silk brocade I had once used in another gown. It had a gold background, which I thought would work well with the pleated metallic organza. I also hoped to find a golden ribbon to complete the look.

The muslin sleeves helped determine the width and placement of the panels that would run down the center of the sleeves. I used a slim, fitted sleeve pattern with an elbow dart and decided to put a short zipper at the base of each sleeve. My original thought had been to have the sleeves lace up, like the back, but after seeing it in muslin, I didn't care for it. I decided upon another treatment: long panels of pleated silk organza, spanned by chains of pearls.

The Sleeves

The base of the sleeves was a sturdy muslin. I used two layers of the metallic silk organza to form a vertical panel

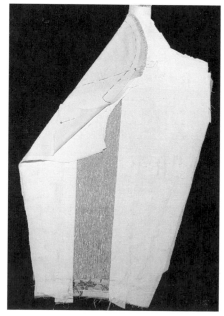

Figure 4-37: The base fabric for these sleeves was muslin, while the center panel in each was made from two layers of pleated metallic organza. The side panels were silk douppioni.

The Center Front and Back Panels

The center front and two center back panels were cut from the embellished silk douppioni. The organza underlining was cut first, and its seamlines were marked with tracing paper. Difficult to see, the marks were gone over with white thread. The organza was used to guide the layout of the douppioni, acting almost like a set of transparent pattern pieces (Figure 4-39). Once cut, the heavy douppioni and the lightweight silk organza were hung vertically in order to be properly aligned; I didn't want any rippling along the edges. Dark thread was used to baste the layers together; it later served as a guide when the ornamentation was cleared from the seam allowances in preparation for stitching.

Figure 4-39: The embellished center front and back panels were underlined with silk organza, which had been traced and staystitched. Although it would later be basted to the wrong side of the embellished douppioni, its transparency was useful when ensuring that the douppioni's motifs were placed attractively.

Figure 4-40: All of the dress panels were underlined with silk organza. Dark thread was used on the embellished panels to serve as a guide when clearing the seam allowances of pearls and beads.

stitching, I carefully checked the ornamentation and filled in any missing areas with discarded beads. A piece of horsehair strengthened the top edge and encouraged it to lie flat against the chest (Figure 4-41).

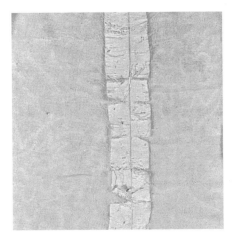

Figure 4-41: Horsehair was used to reinforce the top edge of the front panel so it would lie flat against the upper chest.

In the center of the upper back of the gown, I replicated the proportions of the muslin mock-up: The buttonhole panels were self-faced and underlined with silk organza to make a sturdy base for the buttonholes, and the back panel of silk brocade was underlined with firm cotton organdy.

Before stitching, all ornamentation had to be cleared from the seam allowances of the three long panels. Using the dark basting threads as my guide, I cleared all ornamentation from the seam allowances. It is a long process, because not only does the ornamentation have to be removed, but any remaining unstable embellishments along the seamline and within the body of the dress need to be restitched to prevent further loss.

The Side Front and Side Back Panels

These panels, cut from silk douppioni, were also underlined with silk organza (Figure 4-40). I then reinforced the shoulders of each panel with iron-on interfacing applied to the silk organza underlining. Under normal circumstances, the organza underlining would be sufficient, but the weight of the front and back panels put an enormous amount of strain on the shoulders of the gown. A strip of silk organza selvage strengthened the shoulder seamline as well as the vertical front seamlines above the bust (starting slightly below the point at which the side front panels join the front panel and extending to the shoulder seam). If this had not been done, these slightly off-grain seamlines would have been distorted by the weight of the front panel. I also reinforced the corresponding back seamlines with silk organza selvage.

Stitching the Seams

The heavy center front panel was first basted to each side front panel. After carefully checking that the seamlines hung without puckering, I sewed the side front seams. I stitched the seams with a zipper foot, using a regular stitch length. I stitched slowly, giving the needle a chance to slide to the side of any nearby pearls or beads rather than come down directly on top of them. I positioned my adjustable zipper foot so that its edge was in line with the needle and the seamline. After

Still using the zipper foot, the center back panels of the gown were stitched together after having been carefully basted (Figure 4-42). After stitching, I carefully checked the ornamentation and filled in any missing areas with dis-

Figure 4-42: The embellished douppioni, its seam allowances cleared of ornamentation, was stitched with a regular stitch length. Also, the seam was stitched slowly so the needle could slide to the side of any pearl or bead it encountered.

Figure 4-43: After stitching, the beaded areas of the embellished douppioni were carefully checked; missing areas were filled with discarded beads.

carded beads (Figure 4-43). Then, the upper back panel was basted and stitched on. Then, the side back panels were basted and stitched, leaving them open at the bottom for the metallic organza inserts. As with the front, horsehair strengthened the top edge (Figures 4-44 and 4-45).

The Godets

Openings on the lower part of the side back seams (Figure 4-46) reveal godets of the metallic Fortuny-like pleated organza—visible when the gown is in motion. Strictly speaking, these are not godets but the back panels of box pleats. They look and function more as godets than pleats, though, in part because of their triangular shape. Originally, I tried to insert them in the manner of ordinary godets. This didn't work because of the unstable nature of the pleated metallic organza. Instead, I attached facings to the lower part of the skirt panels (one on the plain douppioni side, one on the embellished douppioni side) and stitched the metallic organza panel to those turned-back facings (Figure 4-47). The instability of the metallic organza still posed a problem, however. Even when I basted the organza to a stay the shape of the facings, it continued to widen and become distorted. After much experimentation, I discovered an iron-on interfacing that held it in place and would not pull away after being handled. The interfaced metallic organza was then stitched to the stay, and the three-layered panel was sewn to the facings, forming, basically, a box pleat.

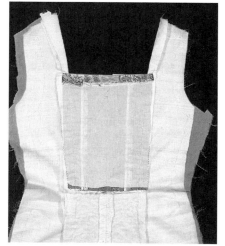

Figure 4-44: A cotton organdy underlining added firmness to the brocade back bodice underlay. Horsehair (not shown) firmed the top edge of the bodice back and was added before the seam allowance was catch stitched in place.

Figure 4-45: An underlay of silk brocade, which also appeared at the base of the sleeves, was used in the artifical back opening. It peeks through the lacing.

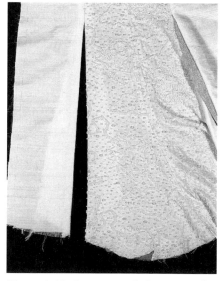

Figure 4-46: Openings on the lower part of the side back seams will reveal godets of the metallic Fortuny-like pleated organza.

Figure 4-47: Facings were attached to the lower edges of the skirt panels (one on the plain douppioni side, one on the embellished douppioni side), and the metallic organza panel was stitched to the outer edges of the facings.

Sewing the Remaining Seams

Once the godets were in place, the side seams were sewn and pressed open. Then the shoulder seams, reinforced with stay tape, were sewn and pressed open.

The Gown's Closure

A zipper placed in the left side seam of the gown runs from the hip area all the way up to under the arm (Figure 4-48). The zipper placket, reinforced with straight-of-grain iron-on tape, had no stretch, but notches made in the seam allowance allowed the zipper to follow the curve of the gown (and of the body).

The Finishing Touches

TRIMMING THE NECK EDGES. I catch stitched the seam allowances of the vertical neck edges in place and then hand sewed tricot-based pearl trim to these edges. The pearl trim quietly echoed both the pearled douppioni and the pearl chains on the sleeves.

HEMMING. I shaped the hem to accommodate the shape and slope of the metallic panels and their facings (Figure 4-49). I stretched a piece of wide horsehair flat along the edge of the hem to stabilize the fishtail and

Figure 4-48: A zipper was placed in the gown's left side seam from the hip to the underarm area. The zipper placket was reinforced with straight-of-grain iron-on tape, and notches in the seam allowance allowed the zipper to follow the curve of the gown.

Figure 4-49: Using horsehair as a stablizer at the fishtail, the hem was shaped to accommodate the shape and slope of the metallic panels and their facings.

then gathered the horsehair slightly to conform to the fishtail shape. Weights were added to either side of the seam openings to encourage the panels to hang straight. I formed a shallow pleat in the lining which encouraged the fishtail to glide smoothly (Figure 4-50).

INSERTING THE LINING. The lining for this gown was easy enough to insert, although it had to be left open along the lower side back seams to accommodate the metallic organza panels. The lining was fell stitched around the neck edge, basted around the armscye, and fell stitched along the zipper.

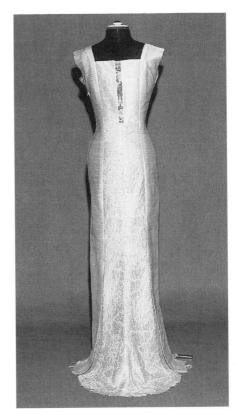

Figure 4-50: Weights were sewn in the hem of the long dress panels, close to the split seam, to encourage the seams to remain closed except when the wearer moved to reveal the metallic panels.

At the lower side back seam split, I aligned the lining with the original lower side back seamline, from the split to the hem, and fell stitched it in place. the facings and the back panels of the pleated organza inserts were left unlined (although they were underlined), and their seam allowances were carefully trimmed and hand overcast.

INSERTING THE SLEEVES. Inserted in the normal manner, a sleeve header was used to fill out and shape the sleeve head area, and a strip of spun silk was used to bind the seam allowance. Bra carriers were sewn in place, and the seam allowance at the shoulder area was tacked toward the neck edge.

LACING THE "OPENING." At Hyman Hendler in New York (see Resources), just the right ribbon was found to lace up the back panel—a final exotic touch that tied the whole dress together. Pearled or antique tassels could be attached to the ends of the ribbon for an elegant accent.

A Glamorous Blue Gown

This is a glamorous gown, with its fitted mini-dress and wraparound detachable skirt. Although the mini-dress is sleek, it was not form-fitting enough to be boned, and simply making it skin-tight wouldn't have kept it in place. The answer was to create an inner corselette that stopped at the waist. The corselette would support the dress because the corselette and the dress would be joined along the top edge. The dress hangs from the snug and well-boned corselette, skimming over the body without evidence of the inner support.

CONSTRUCTION OF THE BLUE GOWN

Fabrication

Visually, this gown and its success depend on the sum of the parts. Although each element is lovely, the effect is compounded when the elements are combined. The mini-dress is fun—very short, tight and sparkly and covered with an unusual Chantilly lace. The net background of the lace is brown, and its motifs are completely covered with silvery-blue sequins. The fabric is lightweight, shimmery, and very unique. The soft, ice-blue taffeta skirt glistens, and ample inner support gives it body and movement (a hidden touch of luxury is its grey silk charmeuse lining). Silk flowers, echoing the colors of the sequins, cluster at the waist. The challenge was to find disparate though complementary items that are interesting enough on their own, but truly stunning when used in combination. None of the three elements overpower, but, pulled together by color and proportion, they become three wonderful parts of a very lovely whole.

The Muslin

I created muslins for the mini-dress and its inner corselette only. Later, experimentation with the satin and various underlinings guided the shape,

sweep, and fullness of the skirt. For the mini-dress, a Butterick pattern for a strapless dress was shortened and reshaped at the hem to accommodate the mock wrap (Figure 4-51). The muslin for the corselette was a waist-length adaptation of the mini-dress pattern with all ease removed (Figure 4-52). The muslins were fit individually, then together (Figure 4-53).

Figure 4-51: The muslin for the mini-dress included a length of lace and a silk flower to help visualize important elements of design and line, including the mock wrap at the front.

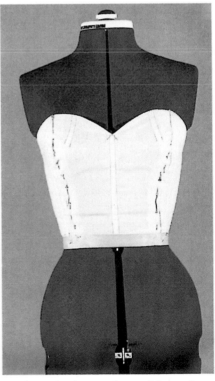

Figure 4-52: The second part of the muslin was the inner corselette, which would support the outer dress.

Figure 4-53: *The two parts of the muslin had to be fit individually, then together.*

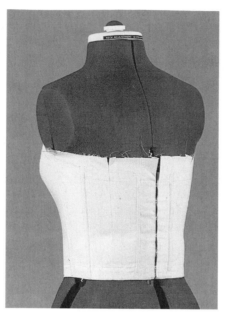

Figure 4-54: *The corselette was made with a double layer of medium-weight cotton. It was adapted from the mini-dress pattern, but it stops at the waist. The boning channels were formed by stitching the two layers of fabric together; separate channels weren't necessary.*

THE MINI-DRESS

For the mini-dress, much experimenting led to a final (and unorthodox) choice of two layers of polyester organza on top of two layers of polyester taffeta (Figure 4-56). Although silk organza and silk taffeta would have been preferable, the colors created by the polyester fabrics in combination worked perfectly. I planned to cover the four layers with lace and line the entire dress with crepe de chine. Would adding the corselette make the garment too thick? No, but I had to take special care that the seams lay absolutely flat and smooth. I also had check the fit of the gown carefully.

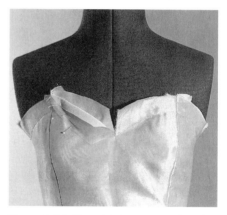

Figure 4-56: *The mini-dress was made with two layers of polyester organza on top of two layers of polyester taffeta.*

On the muslin, the scrap of lace and the silk flower helped me visualize important elements of design and line (see Figure 4-51). The blue satin (which was my starting point for the ensemble), the mini-dress, and the flower needed to be tied together color-wise and design-wise. The skirt could be either pleated or gathered. Since the skirt overlapped slightly, pleats made more sense. They would be flatter and not add bulk at the waistline as satin gathers often do. I decided on a wide waistband which, if cut on the bias, would curve nicely around the waist. Although the white lace scrap pinned to the muslin was far from what the eventual trim would be, it did point the way visually, as did the flower, which would be matched or created later at Dulken and Derrick in New York (see Resources).

Boning channels were formed by stitching through both layers with two parallel rows of stitching; no separate channels had to be created. By self-lining the corselette, I avoided having any raw edges or seam allowances showing. Grosgrain (fitted snugly to the wearer's waist) was placed at the bottom edge of the bodice (Figure 4-55). The unfinished top edge of the bodice was later joined to the top edge of the mini-dress.

Once sewn and pressed, all seam allowances were catch stitched to the taffeta underlining. I stitched twill tape

The Mini-Dress

THE CORSELETTE

The corselette was made with medium-weight cotton (sturdy, and a good choice for absorbing perspiration), which was doubled (Figure 4-54).

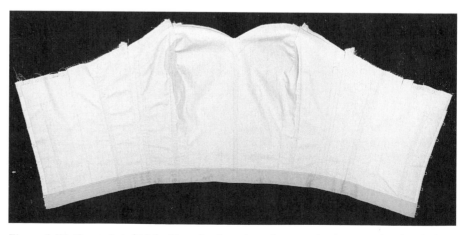

Figure 4-55: *Grosgrain, which had been fitted snugly to the wearer's waist, was placed at the bottom edge of the inner corselette; the unfinished top edge was later joined to the top edge of the mini-dress.*

along the top edge of the bodice (easing in the top edge of the bodice to cup around the bust) and then folded and basted down this edge of the bodice, to help determine lace placement. I did not permanently stitch the edge at this point, because the corselette and lining still had to be sewn in before the lace edging could be applied permanently.

LACE PLACEMENT

In preparation for adding the lace, the mini-dress hem was trimmed and iron-on twill tape was added to stabilize the curves at the front of the hem (Figure 4-57). Because the area to be covered with lace was large, with numerous curves and borders, one wide piece of lace was draped and shaped onto the dress. First, though, because the lace was wider than necessary, the top border was cut off (Figure 4-58). The large piece of lace was positioned so that its lower scalloped border was aligned with the hem of the dress. It was pinned at the widest point—the hipline—to stabilize it. It was pinned frequently to keep it in place, molding and shaping as necessary (Figure 4-59).

Figure 4-58: The lace was wider than necessary, so its top border was cut off and set aside for later use.

Figure 4-57: To get the dress ready for adding the lace, the skirt hem was trimmed and iron-on twill tape was added to stabilize the curves at the front of the hem.

Figure 4-59: The wide piece of lace was pinned at the hipline to hold it in place after the lower lace border was lined up with the hem.

LACE SHAPING

Once the lace was stabilized at the hip- and hemline, it was shaped up onto the bodice. Extra lace was left at the center back seam; it would later be carefully overlapped and stitched, with any bulk removed. With this fairly flexible lace, a combination of stretching and overlapping helped mold it. It didn't need to go all the way to the top, as the lace border would go there. Lots of pins were used, placed in the body of the lace rather than on the delicate net background, which tears easily. I took extra care with the dark net on the light background; multiple layers of net would be obvious, as would ripples and small tears. So, when the net had to be overlapped, I camouflaged the small seam by sewing a row of sequins on top of it. Once the lace had been extensively pinned, the dress was taken off the mannequin and the back seam opened. The dress was placed on a flat surface and the lace was stitched in place. The short back seam was resewn with its lace overlapped and stitched in place.

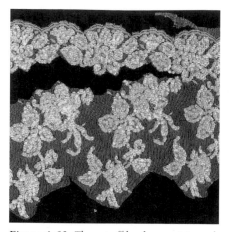

Figure 4-60: The cut-off border was trimmed down further for later use.

MINI-DRESS ASSEMBLAGE

The dress lining, which had to fit smoothly in such a tight-fitting dress, was basted, checked for fit, and then assembled in preparation for insertion along with the corselette. With the back side of the corselette—the side away from the body, that is—against the right side of the lining, I sewed the lining and corselette together (the bones already had been inserted into the corselette). The joined corselette and lining were then sewn to the mini-dress (right sides together). A zipper foot was used to avoid sewing over the bones. Seam allowances were trimmed at this point, as there were so many layers. The seam allowances were clipped frequently and understitched along the top edge of the corselette. Finally, to guarantee no shifting of layers (especially the lining), a prick stitch was applied along the top edge of the dress. The body of the gown was checked for any ripples, tears, or loose threads. The remaining border lace, narrowed further (Figure 4-60), was pieced and shaped up the front of the dress. It continued around both the top edge and the hem so the dress gives the appearance of overlapping at the front (Figure 4-61).

MINI-DRESS FINISHING

To finish the dress, a hand-picked zipper was inserted. The lining was sewn down along the zipper (Figure 4-62). The lining was attached at the hem with a pleat, except at the cutaway at the left front hem, where the lining was fell

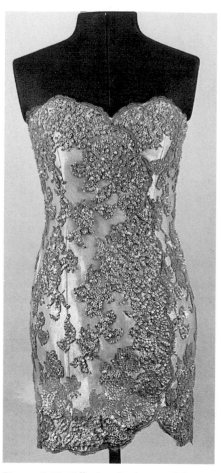

Figure 4-61: Following the shaping of the hem, the narrow strip of border lace continues up the front of the dress, giving the appearance of an overlap. The lace has been pieced and shaped.

Figure 4-62: The lining of the mini-dress was sewn down along the zipper.

stitched in place, then prick stitched to eliminate shifting, pulling, or overhang at the center front (Figure 4-63).

Figure 4-63: From the inside of the mini-dress, the inner corselette is visible. A prick stitch along the top edge keeps layers from shifting.

The Satin Overskirt

SKIRT FABRICATION

The skirt presented the challenge of creating enough inner movement and swing without the benefit of a separate crinoline (separate crinolines don't work with wrap skirts). The skirt's stiffening, therefore, had to be created internally. The satin, doubled to give the skirt more body (this wouldn't have been necessary with a fuller-bodied silk satin), was used lengthwise to eliminate the need for seams. A seam in the back wasn't necessary for shaping or for an opening. The fabrics were combined as follows: two layers of blue polyester satin, one layer of white silk organza (which acts as a buffer for the somewhat stiff cotton organza), one layer of white cotton organza (which does the real shaping), and a grey silk charmeuse lining (Figure 4-64), which is purely decorative and adds a note of luxury. As all the fabrics were used lengthwise, seams and ridges from seam allowances were eliminated.

SKIRT HEMMING AND INNER FINISHING

As all the layers of the skirt were shaped uniformly and consistently, they were hemmed before much of the other finishing work was done. It was easier to hem the layers individually before

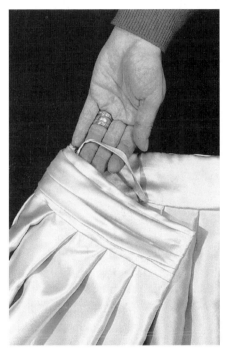

Figure 4-64: The fabrics for the skirts were combined as follows: two layers of blue polyester satin, one layer of white silk organza (which acts as a buffer for the somewhat stiff cotton organza), one layer of white cotton organza (which does the real shaping), and a grey silk charmeuse lining, which is purely decorative and adds a note of luxury. As all the fabrics were used lengthwise, seams and ridges from seam allowances were eliminated.

Figure 4-65: The inside raw edges of the skirts, although not visible from the outside, were bound on each side with strips of silk charmeuse.

reduced bulk. Hanging loops were incorporated into the base of the inner waistband (Figure 4-67). Sturdy hooks and eyes were sewn to the skirt, and silk-covered snaps were added to ensure that the underlap of the waistband stayed in place. Then, a cluster of silk flowers was attached securely to the waistband. Hem weights were placed at the bottom front corners of the skirt, to emphasize a clean, strong vertical line down its front.

Figure 4-67: Hanging loops were incorporated into the base of the inner waistband.

they were joined and gathered. Two-inch-wide horsehair was used to stiffen the hems and shape the skirt. The two layers of satin and the one layer of silk organza act as one (the silk organza functions here as an underlining). I placed horsehair along the hemline so that when the hem folds up, the hem stitches go onto the silk organza. The cotton organza was used as an inner stiffening, but it also had a strip of horsehair inserted at the hem. The silk charmeuse, the innermost layer, was hemmed to itself.

Basting joined all the layers together along their vertical edges; then the charmeuse was used to face them. The inside raw edges, although not visible, still needed to be finished. They were bound on each side with strips of silk charmeuse (Figure 4-65). The layers were then all basted together along the top edge of the skirt and pleated together. Carefully measured, the pleats were firmly stitched by hand. Machine stitching would have distorted the many layers, and shifting would have resulted.

SKIRT FINISHING

A wide grosgrain ribbon was basted to the waistline of the skirt (Figure 4-

66). I placed the ribbon on top of another inner piece of grosgrain that had been stiffened with vertical strips of boning at the center front, side seams, and center back. The satin waistband, draped on the bias, was tacked frequently to maintain its draping. The waistband's lining of silk charmeuse

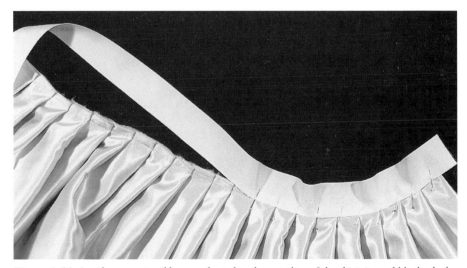

Figure 4-66: A wide grosgrain ribbon was basted to the waistline of the skirt; it would be backed with another inner piece of grosgrain that had been stiffened with vertical strips of boning (at the center front, side seams and center back).

APPENDIX A:
Equipment and Supplies

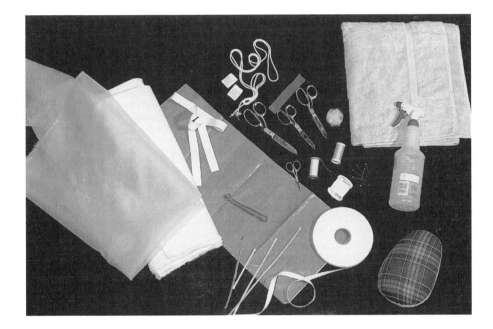

Fine workmanship and fine fabrics need to be paired with first-rate, reliable tools. The task at hand will be easier, and the results will be superior. Poor workmanship cannot be helped by the finest tools and equipment in the world, but quality work deserves the assistance that the best equipment can give. It makes an enormous difference.

Few supplies of a well-equipped atelier fall into the category of high-technology; rather, it is the way in which basic workroom essentials are put to use which makes them so valuable. Further, keeping a supply of these essentials on hand will encourage their use, while broadening one's familiarity with them.

SEWING MACHINE. So much of couture sewing is done by hand that the percentage of time spent at a sewing machine is relatively small. However little the machine is used, though, it must be completely dependable. Rarely is anything more complicated than a straight stitch and occasionally a zigzag called for, but it is the machine's tension and reliability that must be first-rate. Sergers are not used in the couture; their chief attribute, speed, is not an advantage with couture sewing. Serging creates narrow seam allowances (couture uses wide seam allowances, at least during cutting and fitting, and sometimes in the final form of the garment), the seams created by a serger are difficult to take out, and serging very often leaves a ridge along the seam allowance which would be perceptible on the right side of the garment, due to the amount of thread put onto the fabric.

PRESSING EQUIPMENT. A simple dry iron, a spray bottle full of water, a silk organza pressing cloth, a ham, a sleeve board, spray starch and a thick terry towel are the pressing supplies I use regularly. I don't need the steam and pressure of a heavy, professional steam iron for pressing fine silks and other bridal fabrics, and I am always afraid that water will leak from an ordinary steam iron at the wrong time, ruining a garment. Supplying my own water from a spray bottle allows me to control exactly how much moisture I use. I use a ham when pressing over rounded surfaces (princess seams, all darts, side seams which curve) and always use a silk organza pressing cloth. It can tolerate any temperature from the iron, and it's somewhat transparent. Spray starch is useful for stiffening lace, which is pressed face down into a thick towel.

SCISSORS. Nothing undermines the quality of work more quickly than poor scissors, either the wrong size for the job or in poor condition. An array of sizes is necessary—from tiny, sharp ones for hand work, to medium-weight for general use, to large shears. Scissors too small for the job are not only inefficient, they will quickly become overworked and unbalanced; scissors too large for the job will be cumbersome and inaccurate and tiring to use. Serrated blade shears are ideal for cutting silks, because they grab the fabric, making the job much easier and, even more important, more accurate. Replace scissors regularly or have them sharpened professionally.

NEEDLES. With couture's emphasis on hand sewing, a wonderful collection of needles is obviously essential. Beyond the customary sharps, milliner's needles are useful (they are long and thin), as are beading needles (they are very long and very thin and often the only thing that will go through tiny beads).

THREAD. Although different sewers and different sewing machines have their preferences, a long-staple polyester thread is a good place to start. There is much handwork in couture, and it is important that the thread have a good, strong feel, that it not kink up, that it pull evenly and without hesitation through multiple layers of fabric. Silk thread is useful for top basting—it won't leave an impression even if it is pressed. I always use it for basting satin and silk crepe.

BEESWAX. A small but important tool, beeswax coats hand-sewing thread to make it easier to work with and to strengthen it. Waxing is unnecessary for most hand sewing, but it is essential to wax thread when sewing buttons, hooks and eyes, and hand-picked zippers. Coat the thread by pulling it through the beeswax once or twice, and then iron it, to impregnate the fibers with wax.

GLASS-HEADED PINS. When working with lace, not only are glass-headed pins clearly visible in this sometimes thick, three-dimensional fabric, but they won't slip through its net background the way smaller pins do. Further, glass-headed pins push easily through the multiple layers of fabric so often encountered in the course of sewing a gown. Search for and invest in the finest, longest, sharpest glass-headed pins available.

UNBLEACHED MUSLIN. The work-horse of the atelier is unbleached muslin, for it is, quite literally, the canvas on which the artist works. A good supply will encourage the designer to create, and it will allow the dressmaker to work out the fine details of proportion, fit and technique on something other than the fashion fabric. Unbleached muslin is available in a variety of weights; choose a weight compatible with the nature of the garment to be constructed. The cheaper grades of muslin are unstable and will not give an accurate representation of form and fit. Muslin can also be useful as an underlining, but keep in mind its possible effect on the color of the fashion fabric.

TRACING WHEEL AND TRACING PAPER. Couture relies heavily on seam lines and other pattern markings made with tracing paper, instead of predetermined seam allowances and cut-out notches. Marking with tracing paper is relatively quick and completely accurate. It is first the muslin that is marked, and it is this marked set of fabric pieces that become the pattern pieces for the underlining and lining fabrics. Seldom is the fashion fabric marked; with the underlining fully and accurately marked, it isn't necessary. Place the paper pattern and two layers of fabric, pinned together, on top of a single layer of tracing paper. Trace on the paper pattern, then remove the paper pattern, pin the two remaining layers of fabric together, flip them over, and use the just-made markings as a guide for the second set of tracings. Tracing paper is available in a variety of colors. Use a dark color for marking the muslin, for the sake of contrast, but use the lightest one possible with light-colored fabrics. Although difficult to see, white tracing paper must be used with all whites and off-whites.

SILK ORGANZA. Although sometimes used as a fashion fabric, silk organza is usually more useful to the dressmaker for what it can do on the inside of a garment. It is a wonderful underlining, a lightweight and unobtrusive stabilizer, as well as the perfect backing for lace; it adds stability, while maintaining the transparent nature of the lace. White silk organza can easily be dyed with tea or coffee to match skin tones.

BONING. Boning plays an essential role in highly-structured bodices: A well-fitted, generously boned garment is a joy to wear, for the wearer will feel well contained and secure, unaware of what goes on behind the scenes. There are several types of boning available. The most readily available is the heavy plastic type, usually purchased with its

own bias casing; it has the advantage of being able to be cut easily to any length. Also available is a type which can be directly stitched on, without the need for a casing; its chief disadvantage is that once it is applied, it cannot be removed (to be put back in later) while the garment is being worked on. The third type, which is the most versatile of the three, is spiral steel boning, available by the pound as well as pre-cut in lengths from 2 to 17 inches. Spiral steel boning is the strongest of the three, and has the added advantage of lateral movement; it can be curved while maintaining its firm support. It is available from Greenberg and Hammer (see Resources) in New York City.

GROSGRAIN RIBBON. Keep white and off-white grosgrain ribbon on hand in various widths. Use 7/8-inch grosgrain for waistline stays and the narrower widths for other internal stays as well as for hanging loops, boning channels, and bra carriers.

HORSEHAIR. Beyond its customary placement in hems, horsehair's uses are far more wide-ranging, especially in its wider widths: to help maintain a perfect curve in a band sleeve, to stabilize a neck edge, to stiffen bows, to form firm sleeve heads. It's uncrushable, and the shape and support and curve it gives are often impossible to duplicate any other way.

LEAD WEIGHTS: Available either as individual weights or as small pellets encased in a tube, lead weights are a wonderful tool. Beyond their customary use along the hem line of jackets, many gowns benefit from their presence. The hem of a long sheath is a good case for hemline placement of weights (encased in a folded strip of flannel). Further, the lower corners of split seams are a good spot for individual weights (enclosed in small squares of fabric), encouraging the split seam to hang straight.

$\mathscr{A}$PPENDIX B:
Glossary

There are a number of terms and techniques that should be part of the repertoire of any fine dressmaker. Become familiar with them, and practice them, so that you can call upon them as needed. Much of the art of fine dressmaking relies upon the dressmaker's experience and judgment, and it is a thorough knowledge of the craft and its techniques that guides you in making sound, intelligent choices as the project evolves. The following are immensely useful, and their uses wide-ranging.

BACK STITCH. The back stitch, the strongest of the hand stitches, is used to join two layers, or sections, together in a sturdy, straightforward way. If done with double thread coated with beeswax, the back stitch is perfect for joining thick layers together (a gathered sleeve with a thick seam allowance to a lace-covered bodice, or a lace-covered bodice to a gathered, heavy satin skirt, for example). In addition to its strength, it allows for great accuracy.

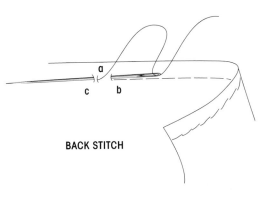

BACK STITCH

BASTING STITCH. Not only is the basting stitch used in the construction process to join the fashion fabric to the underlining, but it is used to baste the garment sections together for fittings. Many fashion fabrics cannot be machine basted for a fitting; the stitch-ing, once removed, is likely to show, and the fabric will suffer from overhandling. After the muslin stage, couture garments are always hand basted, fitted, taken apart, adjusted, and then basted and fitted again several times. Depending on where it's used, the size of the basting stitches can vary; a basted bodice should have fairly small basting stitches in order to replicate a good, tight fit. Basting stitches that are too loose will pull too much and distort the correct fit. Zippers can be basted into garments, hems can be basted in place. Pins in the hem of many fashion fabrics can be ruinous—especially in silk satins and silk crepes; not only will they leave a mark, and possibly a rust spot, but they can snag the fabric. Instead, the hems are basted. Good-quality thread, such as a long-staple polyester, works fine as a basting thread, as does silk. Although expensive, silk thread has the advantage of rarely leaving an impression, even after pressing; it also glides beautifully through thick layers and stubborn fabrics. Seams (especially long ones) are easiest to baste and control if they are spread on a flat surface, with as little fabric distortion as posssible. Basting is most accurate when done exactly on the stitching line, or seamline; of course, it will be more difficult to remove after the seam has been sewn, because, inevitably, some of the basting stitches will have been stitched over, but it is the only way to be completely accurate. Basting outside the seam line will allow for slippage when the seam is machine stitched some distance away. Even if the discrepancy is minimal, there will be slippage, especially with the multiple layers of fabric that are often called for in couture garments. Basting is also used to mark technical details: placement lines, the center front, hemlines, button location. Thread that matches or contrasts slightly with the fashion fabric color can be used, but anything red (or close to it) will leave tiny fibers behind, and anything too contrasting will show if tiny pieces of thread are caught by machine stitching and left behind.

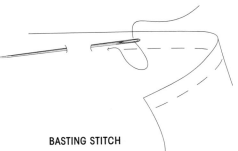

BASTING STITCH

BLANKET STITCH. There are times when the metal of a hook and eye, especially if the hook and eye are of any size, is unsightly; hooks and eyes can easily be covered (before stitching them to the garment) with a blanket stitch. The base of the hook can be spread apart temporarily while it is being covered, then pushed back together. A thread bar can take the place of a metal eye, but a thread-covered metal eye is stronger. Although an extremely fastidious detail, there are times when a hook or eye might be visible, and the gar-

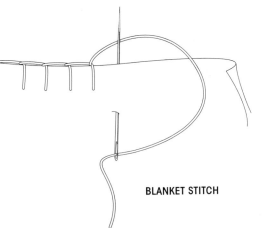

BLANKET STITCH

ment would be marred by the sight of a piece of hardware. Covering it up not only camouflages the metal, but it implies the level of quality with which the whole garment has been addressed.

CATCH STITCH. Another wonderfully useful stitch, the catch stitch is used whenever a layer of fabric (or fabrics) needs to be held flat against another layer. Seam allowances can be opened out and held flat against the underlining with the catch stitch; hems can be stitched with it (it will later be covered up with the lining); it can be used to hold a neckline seam allowance in place. It allows fabrics to be controlled without being pulled, and it has just enough strength to keep layers flat without distortion. Its size is easily adjusted—it can be minutely small and closely spaced, or it can be large and open, covering great distances while still doing its job.

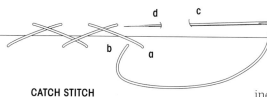

CATCH STITCH

FELL STITCH. The fell stitch is a very useful stitch. Easy and quick to do, it's also sturdy and attractive. It is the perfect way to join one edge to another, especially if, as in the case of applying a lining, the lining is placed just inside the edge of the fashion fabric. The advantage of the fell stitch, in addition to being secure and tight, is that hardly any thread appears on the top side of the stitch. Not only is this an advantage for cosmetic reasons, nothing is left to snag or catch. It is the stitch used to secure the lining to the zipper, to sew on lace appliqués, to attach the bias casing around the armscye, to finish off

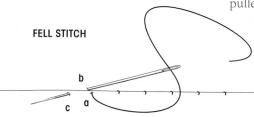

FELL STITCH

the bias piping at a neckline or elsewhere, to stitch the lining down not only around the top edge but down the back opening and at the base of the bodice.

FRENCH TACK. A French tack is formed by a length of chain stitches. The thread, which is stronger if coated with beeswax, is anchored to the starting point, the thread chain is created, and then it is anchored to the finishing point. Among other uses, it can join layers of a skirt together intermittently at the hemline, it can be used to make lingerie straps, and it can be used to create belt loops.

GATHERING. Gathering works most successfully when done with three layers of gathering stitches. The correct stitch size requires experimentation— the smaller the better, but not so small that the stitches are frustrating to work with and apt to break. If the gathering stitches are too large, the gathers won't be held in place firmly enough, and they will slip out of place and lose their beauty. If thick seam allowances must be incorporated in the gathers (and inevitably they will, when gathering gown skirts), the thread must be able to be gathered there, too. The threads on the wrong side of the fabric are usually those which are pulled, but there are times when tiny, well-regulated gathers are partciularly prominent, and pulling the threads on the fashion fabric side may give better results. In either case, the first row of gathering stitches is sewn on the stitching line, and the second and third are sewn in the seam allowance. Once the gathering stitches are pulled, the gathers should be worked back and forth until they are manageable. The three rows of thread must be identically pulled; the gathers should resemble tiny cartridge pleats with the seam allowances in line and the tiny pleats perpendicular to the seamline. Once the gathers are properly lined up, the seam allowance can be pressed to

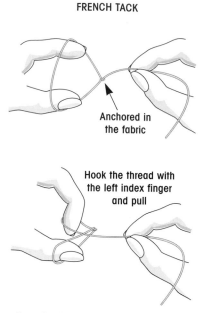

Anchored in the fabric

Hook the thread with the left index finger and pull

Drop the thread from the left thumb, then join the left thumb and left index fingers together inside the index finger's thread loop. Pull until the first loop forms on the surface of the fabric.

Repeat the steps again and again until the chain is the desired length.

Finish by drawing the thread through the final loop.

flatten the gathers and reduce bulk. Just as importantly, pressing will encourage the gathers to stay in place while they are being stitched. First, baste them carefully into place, then machine stitch them.

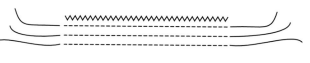

GATHERING STITCH

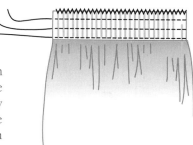

GLAZING. This is an undesirable shine that appears when a fabric has been pressed at too high a heat, or without a pressing cloth, or with excessive pressure. Some fabrics are more prone to glazing than others (linen glazes easily, for example, because of the high heat needed to press it, and because of its natural wax content). Glazing can be avoided by using a pressing cloth, by pressing on the wrong side of the fabric, by ironing at the correct temperature and by using the correct amount of pressure.

HAND OVERCASTING.

Hand overcasting is the quintessential couture edge-finishing stitch. Clean, neat, and evenly spaced, well-regulated hand overcasting stitches are in a class by themselves when it comes to finishing a seam allowance. There is nothing that can take the place of hand overcasting; a machine zigzag creates a thick ridge and often allows multiple layers of fabric within the seam allowance to shift; a Hong Kong finish can be thick and less than perfectly straight; pinking is unsightly and can show through; a French seam can be stiff and bulky (interrupting the flow of the garment); folding the seam allowance under and stitching it forms a ridge and can easily distort an off-grain seam. Hand overcasting, although somewhat time-consuming, is the only option that creates none of these problems. There is no bulk, nor is there ever a ridge; there is no show-through, and the stitch doesn't pull at the seam allowance and distort it (a critical consideration with long, off-grain skirt seams). Furthermore, hand overcasting allows for any layers to be held firmly in place without shifting and slipping. It does the job efficiently and unobtrusively and is one of the hallmarks of a beautifully finished garment.

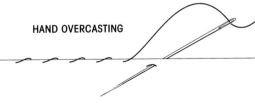

HAND OVERCASTING

INVISIBLE HEM STITCH.

Also called the blind stitch, the invisible hem stitch is a hemming stitch in which the thread is hidden between the hem and the fashion fabric. The two layers are joined

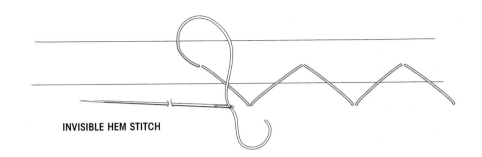

INVISIBLE HEM STITCH

by a row of stitches that zigzags from one side to the other, taking tiny bites out of the fabrics as it goes along. It is never pulled tight, and is a very gentle, inconspicuous way to hem light- to medium-weight fabrics. Sometimes a catch stitch is used in the same way and hidden between the hem and the fashion fabric; the catch stitch creates slightly stronger stitches.

PRESSING.

Careful pressing is an essential component of the success of any garment, and it must be done correctly throughout the construction process. Experimentation early on is the key to knowing the fabrics' reactions to heat, moisture, steam, and pressure. There are often numerous fabrics within a garment, and they will all react differently. A good pressing cloth is essential, even when working on a fabric's wrong side. Silk organza is a good choice—not only is it transparent, it can take the highest heat settings. After stitching, seams must first be pressed flat, still unopened, to meld the stitches. Pressure is applied straight down, without moving the iron or shifting the fabric. The seams are then opened (they can be spread apart with a fingernail). It is critical, especially when multiple layers are involved, that the seam be fully spread; otherwise, small creases will inevitably be pressed in and they are impossible to remove. Thirdly, the seam is pressed, taking care not to distort, overpress, or scorch the fabric. Fine fashion fabrics are seldom pressed on the right side; it is too easy for underlayers or the hem to show through, for the fabric to glaze, or for a crease to sneak in. Steam and pressure are not essential components in the pressing of these fine (and often

delicate) fabrics the way they are with tailoring; a gown can be ruined with moisture and too much pressure from the iron. As always, experimentation is the key.

PRICK STITCH.

The prick stitch is a neat, strong stitch and the perfect way to apply a zipper. It combines strength with control. It is a form of the back stitch, but very little thread appears on the surface. It appears very delicate, with only tiny pricks of thread indicating its presence. It is also invaluable for anchoring a lining at the top of a bodice; after the lining has been applied with a fell stitch, a prick stitch will anchor the lining and keep it from shifting up and becoming visible. In this case, the thread goes through all the layers of fabric except the outermost. It is a wonderful, unobtrusive, but strong tool.

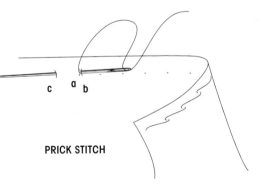

PRICK STITCH

SLIP BASTING.

A particular use of the slip stitch in which a seam is basted from the right side. It is useful with particularly slippery seams, especially if they are curved (a satin princess seam, for example), or if a plaid or other design has to be carefully matched. One edge is turned back along the seamline; this folded edge is pinned in place against the coordinating seamline, and the two edges are slip stitched together. Slip basting securely joins the layers and marks the stitching line.

SLIPPAGE. The tendency of fabrics to slip out of position, slippage can be caused by fabric weight, fabric thickness, natural tendencies, insufficient pinning or basting, or pressure from the sewing machine's presser foot. Control needs to be built in with adequate basting to secure areas before they are stitched. Pins often do not adequately hold thick layers and slippery fabrics in place.

SLIP STITCH. The slip stitch is the most invisible of the hand stitches. It is not particularly strong, but it is perfect for cases when two layers need to be joined in a flat and unobtrusive manner. It works well as a hem stitch (it is perfect for sheer fabrics that have a deep hem). The stitches are hidden in the fold of the hem fabric, and only tiny stitches appear on the outside before the thread disappears again.

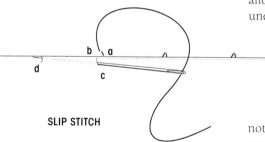

SLIP STITCH

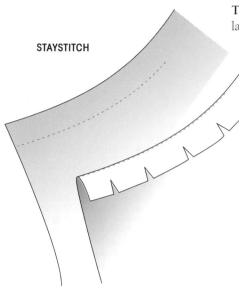

STAYSTITCH

STAYSTITCH. It is important to stabilize edges that curve or are off grain. Staystitching, which is a line of machine stitching along a seamline or foldline, will not only discourage a seam from stretching, but it will firm and help define curved seam allowances that will later be turned under (the neck edge of a lining, for example, which has to be clipped, turned and pressed before being fell stitched into place). Staystitching will not only stabilize the edge, but it will serve as a stitching guide. The seam allowance is turned so that the stitching is on the inside of the folded edge, just barely beyond view. Some seams which are stay stitched will be further stabilized with the application of twill tape (diagonal bodice lines and shoulder seams, for example).

THREAD BAR. The thread bar is similar to a French tack, but much stronger. Multiple threads are secured in place and then covered with blanket or buttonhole stitches. The stitch creates a strong, neat, sturdy bar—perfect for the loops used to bustle a skirt, for a button loop at a back neck closure, or for a thread eye for a metal hook.

THREAD BAR

Reinforced underneath with a square of bias-cut silk organza, if used as a bustling loop

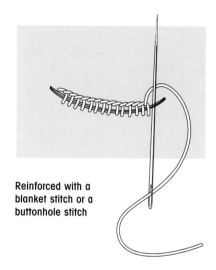

Reinforced with a blanket stitch or a buttonhole stitch

APPENDIX C:
A Guide to Pronunciation

The following is a guide to some of the more commonly-used terms used in connection with bridal fabrics; most of them are French in origin.

Alençon—ah-lehn-sahn´

Chantilly—shan-til´-ee

Douppioni—doo-pee-ohn´-ee

Faille—fyle

Grosgrain—groh´-grayn

Guipure—gih-pyuhr´

Moiré—mwaah-ray´

Schiffli—shihf´-lee

Soutache—soo´-tash

Toile—twahl

Tulle—tool

Valenciennes—val-ehn-see-enn´

Venise—veh-neez´

$\mathcal{A}$PPENDIX D:
Resources

There are now a number of wonderful mail-order fabric resources, essential to anyone distant from a source of fine fabrics. In addition, here are a select few resources which are unique and invaluable to the couture dressmaker. I have been dealing with all of them for years, and treasure their presence, their level of service, and their commitment to quality.

Dulken and Derrick
12 W. 21st St., 6th Floor
New York, New York 10010
(212) 929-3614

A treasure-trove of silk flowers, from the antique to the new to the custom-made; the scope and quality of their stock is breathtaking, and unequalled.

Greenberg and Hammer, Inc.
24 West 57th Street
New York, New York 10019
(800) 955-5135

A source of notions and dressmaking supplies, from the standard to the obscure. They stock spiral steel boning, along with everything else that goes inside a garment. A mail order catalogue is available.

Hyman Hendler and Sons
67 West 38th Street
New York, New York 10018
(212) 840-8393

A shop devoted to ribbons; the variety, the charm, the inspiration are endless, and the quality of their ribbons, most of which are European, is superb.

APPENDIX E:
Suggested Reading

There is little in print which specifically addresses bridal sewing, but there are a number of wonderful resources for both broader technical advice on a high level, as well as inspiration on a grand scale. For the dressmaker about to embark on any special sewing project, they provide know-how, encouragement and inspiration. Among them are:

FOR TECHNICAL ADVICE:

Carr, Roberta C. *Couture: The Art of Fine Sewing*. Portland, OR, Palmer/Pletsch Incorporated, 1993.

Shaeffer, Claire B. *Claire Shaeffer's Fabric Sewing Guide, Updated Edition*. Radnor, PA: Chilton Book Company, 1994.

Shaeffer, Claire B. *Couture Sewing Techniques*. Newtown, CT, The Taunton Press, 1993.

FOR INSPIRATION:

Assouline, Prosper. *Haute Couture—Tradesman's Entrance*. Paris, France: Editions Assouline, 1990.

Cullerton, Brenda. *Geoffrey Beene*. New York: Harry N. Abrams, Inc., 1995.

Jacobs, Laura. *The Art of Haute Couture*. New York: Abbeville Press, 1995.

Kirke, Betty. *Madeleine Vionnet*. Tokyo: Kyuryudo Art Publishing Co., Ltd., 1991.

Martin, Richard and Koda, Harold. *Flair: Fashion Collected by Tina Chow*. New York: Rizzoli International Publications, 1992.

Martin, Richard and Koda, Harold. *Haute Couture*. New York: The Metropolitan Museum of Art and Harry N. Abrams, Inc., 1995.

McBride-Mellinger, Maria. *The Wedding Dress*. New York: Random House, 1993.

Milbank, Caroline Rennolds. *Couture: The Great Designers*. New York: Stewart, Tabori and Chang, 1985.

Stewart, Martha. *Weddings*. New York: Clarkson N. Potter, 1987.

Train, Susan, ed. *Théâtre de la Mode*. New York: Rizzoli International Publications, 1991.

Valentino: Thirty Years of Magic (Exhibition Catalogue). Milan: Gruppo Editoriale Fabbri, Bompiani, Sonzogno, Etas S.p.A., 1992.

White, Palmer. *Haute Couture Embroidery: The Art of Lesage*. Berkeley, CA: Lacis Publications, 1994.

Wilcox, Claire and Mendes, Valerie. *Modern Fashion in Detail*. Woodstock, NY: The Overlook Press, 1991.

ABOUT THE AUTHOR

photo by June Chaplin

Susan Khalje, originally a classical pianist, received her couture training at the New York establishment Chez Cez et Bez. She later served as a designer and manufacturing supervisor for the ladies' sportswear firm ISIS, based on 7th Avenue in New York.

After living in Afghanistan and Europe, she returned to Baltimore and began developing an appreciative clientele for her one-of-a-kind gowns. In addition to writing, she teaches couture sewing techniques across the country and at week-long seminars held periodically in Baltimore, Maryland, and Portland, Oregon.

A charter member of the Professional Association of Custom Clothiers (PACC), she currently serves as its national Chairperson.

She lives on a farm north of Baltimore with her husband and two children.

For more information on Susan Khalje's week-long couture sewing seminars, contact The Bridal Sewing School, P.O. Box 51, Long Green, Maryland 21092.